Santillana Spotlight on English

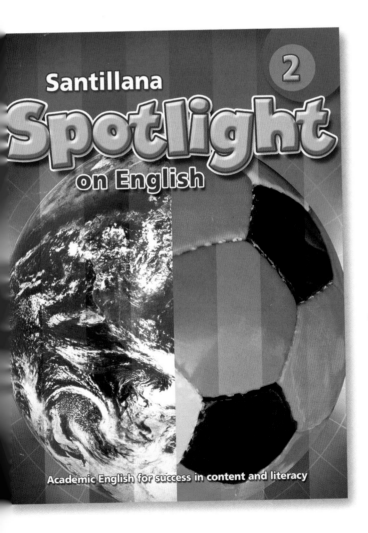

Academic English for success in content and literacy

STUDENT BOOK 2

Published in the United States of America.

Santillana Spotlight on English
Student Book Level 2
ISBN-13: 978-1-59820-734-7
ISBN-10: 1-59820-734-2

Editorial Staff
Editorial Director: Mario Castro
Developmental Editors: Lourdes M. Cobiella, Jill Korot, Patrice Titterington, Patricia Acosta
Design and Production Manager: Mónica R. Candelas Torres
Design and Layout: Nancy Ortega, Erika González, Patricia Reyes
Image and Photo Research Editor: Mónica Delgado
Cover Design and Layout: Studio Montage
Cover Photograph: © Rachel Royse / Corbis

Santillana USA Publishing Company, Inc.
2105 NW 86th Avenue, Miami, FL 33122

Printed in Colombia by Quebecor World Bogotá.

12 11 10 09 08   1 2 3 4 5 6 7 8 9 10

Acknowledgments:
Illustrations: Alejandra Lunik, Marcela Alejandra Calderón, Marcela Lescarboura, Mariano Epelbaum, Mima Castro, Valeria Rodríguez do Campo

Photographs: p.6-7: © Bruce Burkhardt / Corbis; p.24: © David Woods / Corbis, © Hutchings Stock Photography / Corbis, © Jim Craigmyle / Corbis; p.25: © Gabe Palmer / Corbis, © Hutchings Stock Photography / Corbis, © William Gottlieb / Corbis; p.26: © Jose Luis Pelaez, Inc. / Corbis; p.34: © H&S Produktion / Corbis; p.36-37: © Ariel Skelley / Corbis; p.51: © Michael Prince / Corbis; p.53: © Michael Prince / Corbis, © Tamara Reynolds / Corbis; p.64: © Ariel Skelley / Corbis; p.66-67: © Rob Lewine / Corbis; p.96-97: © Bryn Colton/Assignments Photographers / Corbis; p.97: © Duomo / Corbis; p.113: © Birgid Allig/ zefa / Corbis, © Envision / Corbis, © Norbert Schaefer / Corbis,

© Rick Gomez / Corbis; p.120: © FK PHOTO / Corbis, © Lester Lefkowitz / Corbis, © Macduff Everton / Corbis, © Mark E. Gibson / Corbis, © Penny Tweedie / Corbis, © Tim Pannell / Corbis, © Philip Gendreau Bettmann / Corbis, © Roy Morsch / Age Fotostock America; p.121: © Ed Bock / Corbis, © Randy Faris / Corbis, ©LWA-Dann Tardif / Corbis; p.123: © Images.com / Corbis; p.124: © Bryn Colton/Assignments Photographers / Corbis; p.126-127: © Jose Fuste Raga / Corbis; p.142: © Gabe Palmer / Corbis, © Henry Diltz / Corbis, © Jeffery Allan Salter / Corbis, © Ronnie Kaufman / Corbis; p.146: © Tom Stewart / Corbis, © Tom Stewart / Corbis; p.150: © Craig Tuttle / Corbis, © Jean-Pierre Lescourret / Corbis; p.151: © Bo Zaunders / Corbis, © John Gillmoure / Corbis, © Grand Tour / Corbis; p.156-157: © Hans Strand / Corbis; p.158: © Don Mason / Corbis, © Gray Hardel / Corbis, © Ron Watts / Corbis, © Warren Morgan / Corbis, © NASA / Corbis; p.160: © Liang Zhuoming / Corbis, © WildCountry / Corbis; p.161: © Jim Sugar / Corbis; p.162: © Mark M. Lawrence / Corbis, © Stuart Westmorland / Corbis; p.163: © Jose Fuste Raga / Corbis, © NASA / Corbis; p.164: © Kazuyoshi Nomachi / Corbis, © Phil Banko / Corbis; p.166: © Buddy Mays / Corbis, © PNC/zefa / Corbis; p.168: © Bob Krist / Corbis, © Creasource / Corbis, © George H. H. Huey / Corbis, © Theo Allofs / Corbis, © Tony Waltham/Robert Harding World Imagery / Corbis, © Walter Geiersperger / Corbis; p.170: © NASA / Corbis, © Visuals Unlimited / Corbis, Age Fotostock America; p.171: © Ariel Skelley / Corbis, © Carl & Ann Purcell / Corbis, © G. Baden/zefa / Corbis, © LWA-Dann Tardif / Corbis, © Poppy Berry/zefa / Corbis, © Tom Stewart / Corbis; p.173: © Andrew Sacks / Corbis, © Ariel Skelley / Corbis, © Grace/zefa / Corbis, © Mark Seelen/zefa / Corbis; p.176: © Angelo Cavalli/zefa / Corbis, © Pedro Costa/epa / Corbis; p.178: © Photomorgana / Corbis, © Randy Wells / Corbis; p.180: © Birgid Allig/zefa / Corbis, © Jeffrey Green/Veer / Corbis, © Richard Hutchings / Corbis; p.182: © Craig Tuttle / Corbis, © Gary Bell/zefa / Corbis; p.183: © Corbis; p.186-187: © Frans Lanting / Corbis; p.188: © Gary Bell/zefa / Corbis, © Arthur Morris / Corbis, © David Aubrey / Corbis, © Larry Williams / Corbis; p.189: © DLILLC / Corbis; p.194: © Jonathan Blair / Corbis; p.211: © Corbis; p.214: © Ariel Skelley / Age Fotostock America; p.216-217: © Bettmann / Corbis, © Bettmann / Corbis, © Corbis, © Flip Schulke / Corbis, © Louise Gubb / Corbis, © Owaki/ Kulla / Corbis, © Rufus F. Folkks / Corbis; p.233: © Ron Watts / Corbis; p.236: © Bettmann / Corbis; p.237: © Corbis; p.240: © Brooklyn Museum / Corbis; p.241: © Bettmann / Corbis; p.242: © Bettmann / Corbis, © Bettmann / Corbis, © Deborah Betz Collection / Corbis, © Bettmann / Corbis; p.244: © Cardinale Stephane / Corbis SYGMA; p.245: © Ga-len Rowell/ Corbis, © Neal Preston / Corbis

Table of Contents

Santillana Spotlight on English

2

Unit 1 My School

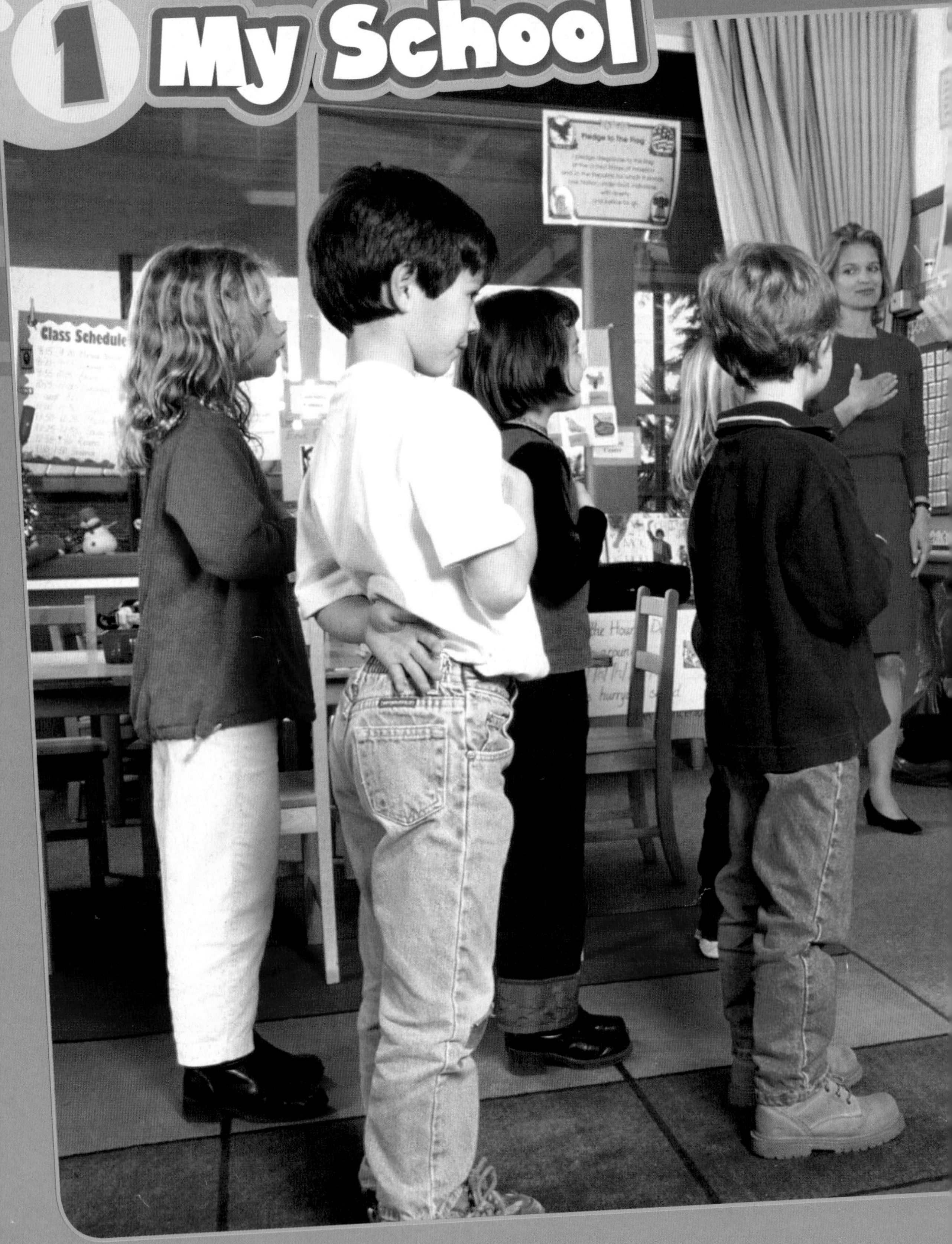

The Pledge of Allegiance
We recite every day.
We hold our hands to our hearts
To show we mean what we say.
Teacher calls one student
To hold the flag up high,
As the class makes a promise
That begins with the word "I."

I will learn to talk about …

▸ school subjects

▸ school locations

▸ school activities

▸ personal preferences

Spotlight on Reading

Key Words

crayon

watercolors

school bus

plant

instruments

Let's Predict!

▶ Answer the questions.

1. What will this story be about?

2. What does the title of the story tell you?

3. What clues do the Key Words provide to what might happen in the story?

4. What fun things will the students do at school?

Fun at School

by Tatiana Sildus
Illustrated by Alejandra Lunik

My name is Naseem. I am in second grade.
I have many friends in my class. My friends
and I like school.

This is my friend. Her name is Ebony. She is good at adding numbers on the board. She likes math. We count numbers in math. We learn to add and subtract, too. Sometimes we play store and pretend to buy and sell things.

This is Mario. He likes art. He likes to draw and paint animals. We use colored pencils and crayons for art. Sometimes we paint with paintbrushes and watercolors.

This is Li-Lei. She likes to read books. We have lots of books in our classroom. Our teacher reads to us every day. There are many interesting books in the school library, too. What is your favorite book?

This is Matt. He likes to go on field trips. Matt likes to see new things. Our class takes the school bus. We visit different places during our field trips. We learn a lot.

My classmates and I like to help our teacher at school. We water our plant every week. We feed our fish in the aquarium. We also take care of our small turtle. It is 20 years old!

I like to play with friends at recess. We play on the playground. The playground has a slide and some swings. Sometimes we play games. Hopscotch is our favorite game.

My friends and I like music. We listen to
music and learn songs. Sometimes we play
instruments, like drums. We have fun in
music class.

I think school is great! My classmates and I learn together. We also play together. Our school is a happy place.

Let's Check!

▶ Choose the correct answers.

1. What place does Naseem describe in the story?
   a. a store   b. a school   c. a park

2. In what grade is Nasseem?
   a. first grade   b. second grade   c. third grade

3. Who likes field trips?
   a. Li-Lei   b. Ebony   c. Matt

4. What does Naseem like to do at recess?
   a. read books   b. play with friends   c. sing songs

5. How do students travel on field trips?
   a. by school bus   b. by car   c. by plane

Let's Retell!

A Use the pictures to talk about what Naseem does at school.

B Write a paragraph about what Naseem likes to do at school.

read books   play with friends   paint with watercolors
learn songs   add and subtract

Let's Reflect!

A Tell a classmate what you like about school.

B Draw a picture of one thing you like to do at school.

Spotlight on Language

Let's Connect!

A Listen and point to the students as they speak.

B Use the dialogue to introduce yourself to a classmate.

Let's Focus!

▶ Copy and complete the sentences.

I   He   She   My   His   Her

1. _____ name is Lupita.

2. _____ am in second grade.

3. _____ name is Naseem.

4. _____ is seven years old.

5. _____ is their teacher.

6. _____ name is _____.

Let's Apply!

Ⓐ Ask your classmates questions. Find someone who …

1. is eight years old.

2. is seven years old.

3. has a name that starts with the same letter as yours.

4. has a brother or sister in fifth grade.

Ⓑ Write two or three sentences about your classmates. Report back to the class.

Paul is eight years old.

Luisa is …

Let's Connect!

Ⓐ Listen and sing.

> Today I need a ruler,
>   A ruler, a ruler.
> Today I need a ruler,
>   To measure a plant.
>
> My friend gives me a ruler,
>   A ruler, a ruler.
> My friend gives me a ruler.
>   I measure a plant.

Ⓑ Sing the song again using these objects.

a pencil – to write down my name

a crayon – to draw a gray cat

a pair of scissors – to cut pictures out

an eraser – to erase mistakes

Let's Focus!

▶ Copy and complete the sentences.

a	an

1. I need _____ ruler.

2. I need _____ crayon.

3. I need _____ eraser.

4. He gives me _____ pair of scissors.

5. He gives me _____ pencil.

Let's Apply!

A Write a list of supplies you need for school.

B Draw and color pictures of the objects on your list.

C Write a sentence describing each school object.

D Bind the pictures to make a school-supplies booklet.

I need a pencil to write stories.

Let's Connect!

A Listen and point to the correct person.

B Talk about what the people above do.

Let's Focus!

▶ Copy and complete the sentences with the correct words.

1. I _____ a principal.　(am / is)

2. The nurse _____ in the nurse's office.　(work / works)

3. I am a librarian. I _____ about books.　(talk / talks)

4. She _____ a food server.　(am / is)

5. The principal _____ many papers on her desk.　(have / has)

Let's Apply!

A Visit the nurse's office, the principal's office, the cafeteria, and the library with your teacher. Find out the names of the school workers in each of these places.

B Write a paragraph about one of the school workers.

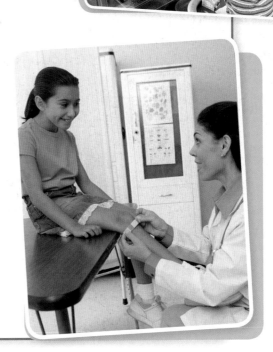

Spotlight on Content

Personal Profile

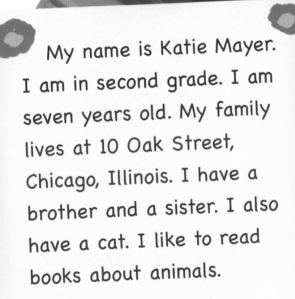

My name is Katie Mayer. I am in second grade. I am seven years old. My family lives at 10 Oak Street, Chicago, Illinois. I have a brother and a sister. I also have a cat. I like to read books about animals.

▶ Answer the questions.

1. Who wrote this paragraph? How do you know?

2. What is the first piece of information the writer includes?

3. What is the second piece of information?

Writing a Personal Profile

> Personal profiles give information about a person. You can write a profile about yourself or about another person. Remember to include this information about the person:
> - first and last name
> - school
> - age
> - home
> - family
> - interests

A Complete a mind map about yourself.

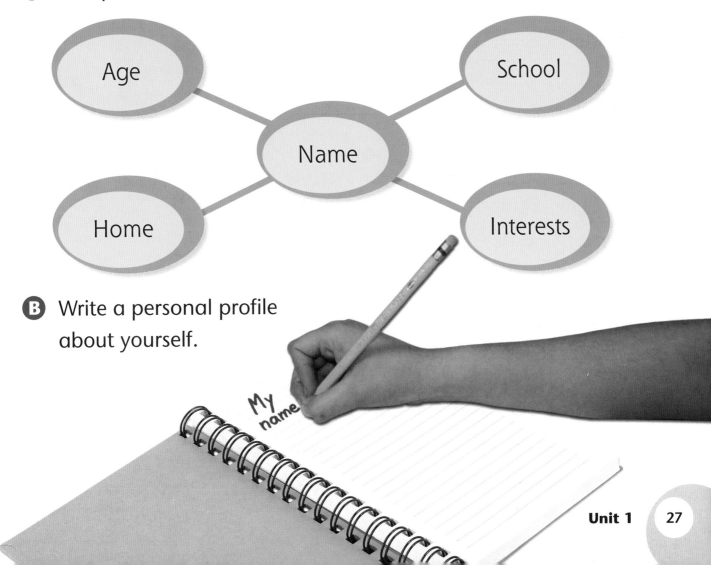

Age

School

Name

Home

Interests

B Write a personal profile about yourself.

My name

Types of Sentences

A sentence is a group of words that expresses a complete idea. There are different types of sentences.

Some sentences give information.
These sentences end with a period (.).
My name is Maggie.

Some sentences ask for information.
These sentences end with a question mark (?).
What is your name?

Some sentences express feelings. These sentences end with an exclamation point (!).
That is beautiful!
Watch out!

All sentences start with a capital letter.

A Read the sentences and decide what types of sentences they are.

1. How old are you

2. School is fun

3. Mario likes to help the teacher

B Copy and complete the sentences with the correct punctuation.

Number Sentences

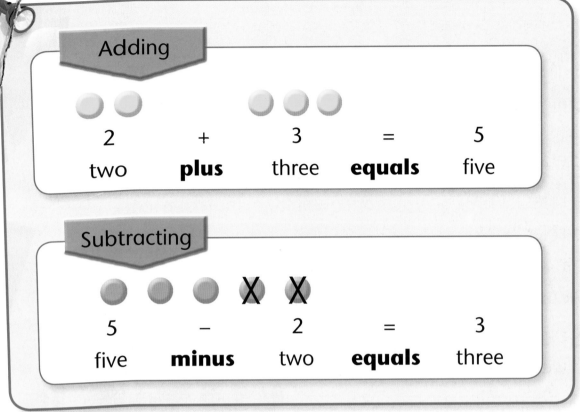

A Answer the questions by counting out loud.

1. How many students are there in your class?

2. How many windows are there in your classroom?

3. How many desks are there in your classroom?

4. How many plants are there in your classroom?

B Solve the problems. Read the number sentences aloud.

1. $7 + 1 =$ _____

2. $6 - 2 =$ _____

3. $3 + 4 =$ _____

4. $10 - 5 =$ _____

5. $9 - 8 =$ _____

6. $2 + 5 =$ _____

School Rules

Every school has rules. They help keep the school an orderly and safe place. All students must follow these rules. Which of these rules do you have at school?

Be on time.

Always walk in the halls.

Take turns.

Leave toys at home.

Throw trash in trash can.

Talk quietly in the cafeteria.

A Read the sentences. Say which students are following the rules.

1. Jack and Chin-Yi take turns on the slide.

2. Amy and David throw trash on the floor.

3. Nick walks to the cafeteria.

4. Alicia leaves her teddy bear at home.

5. Ben and Tom are yelling in the library.

B Make a list of the rules for your classroom.

Plants

There are many different kinds of plants. Some plants grow indoors. Some plants grow outdoors. Plants have roots, a stem, and leaves. Some plants have flowers. Some plants give fruit. Many plants need water, sunlight, and soil.

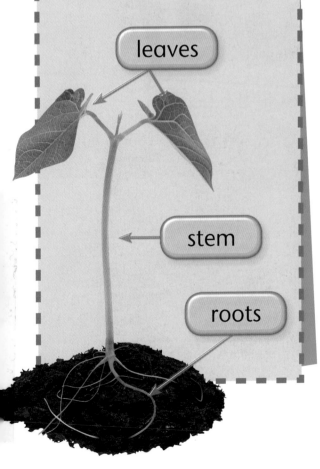

leaves

stem

roots

A Observe a plant in your class. Copy the table and write your observations in the empty column.

Number of leaves	
Color of leaves	
Number of flowers	
Color of flowers	

B Draw a picture of the plant.

C Label the parts of the plant.

Sing Along

A Listen and sing.

School Is Fun!

Some students like drawing and painting.
Some students like problems and games.
Some students like running and jumping.
And others like spelling their names.

School is fun! School is fun!
Students are here to learn, to learn.
School is fun! School is fun!
Students are here to learn!

B Sing the song again. Use the activities in the box.

dancing and singing	reading and writing
playing and laughing	learning new things

Geometric Shapes

Piet Mondrian

Piet Mondrian was a Dutch painter. He used rectangles in his paintings. A rectangle is a geometric shape. Other geometric shapes are squares, circles, and triangles. Mondrian used solid black lines in his paintings. He also used primary colors. Primary colors are red, blue, and yellow.

A Paint your own Mondrian painting.

Supplies

- white paper
- red, yellow, and blue paint
- black marker
- ruler

Steps

1. Draw straight lines to form a rectangle. Use the black marker and the ruler to draw your rectangle.

2. Use the primary colors to paint in different rectangles.

3. Remember to sign your painting!

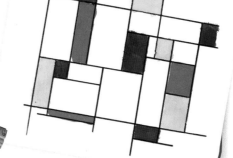

B Share your Mondrian painting with the class.

Hopscotch

Hopscotch is a popular playground game. Children often play it at recess. One student throws a marker onto the first number in the pattern. Then, he or she hops to the end of the pattern and back, picking up the marker on the way back. Players take turns. Some children use this rhyme to see who goes first:

Eenie, meenie, miny, moe.
Catch a tiger by the toe.
If he hollers, let him go.
Eenie, meenie, miny, moe.

▶ Discuss and share.

1. Do children play a similar game in your country?

2. How is it played?

3. What other playground games do they play?

4. Do they use rhymes?

5. What rhymes do you know?

School Location Signs

▶ Make a school location sign.

Supplies

- construction paper
- markers or crayons
- scissors
- old magazines
- glue stick

Steps

1. Draw and color a picture of a location you like to visit in your school.

2. Write the name of the location at the top of the page.

3. Cut and glue pictures of people or objects that you can find at this location.

4. Show your sign to the class and explain why that is your favorite location.

5. Hang your sign in a hallway to show the location.

Unit 2

My Friends and I

While riding your bikes,
Hugging your dolls,
Taking a hike,
Or tossing some balls,
Friends make you feel happy.
They can make you feel sad.
Friends are truly fun to be with.
Doesn't that make you glad?

I will learn to talk about ...

▸ people

▸ feelings

▸ likes and dislikes

▸ clothing

Spotlight on Reading

Key Words

pajamas

toys

race car

security guard

Let's Predict!

▶ Answer the questions.

1. What does the title tell you about the story?

2. Where are the boy and his mother going?

3. What do you think will happen?

4. How do you think the boy will feel?

LOST!

by Tatiana Sildus

Illustrated by Marcela Calderón

Jaime is excited! He is going to his friend's house for a sleepover party. His mom is taking him to a store. They are going to buy some new pajamas.

At the store, Jaime's mom reminds him
to stay safe.

"Stay with me, Jaime. Don't wander off!
We'll get your pajamas first. Then, we can
look at the toys."

There are lots of pajamas.

"Look, Jaime! Here are some pajamas with trucks," says Jaime's mom. "I don't like trucks," says Jaime. "I like race cars."

Jaime's mom looks and looks.

Jaime sees a friend from school.
"Hi, Jaime!" says David. "Let's go look
at the toy race cars."
Jaime and David walk to
the toy department.

"What about these pajamas?" asks Jaime's mom. "They have baseball players on them." She looks around. Oh no! Jaime is gone.

Jaime's mom is worried. She
runs over to the security guard.
"I can't find my son!" says
Jaime's mom.
"Don't worry," says the guard.
"We'll find him."

"What does he look like?" asks the guard.
"He's seven years old. He has brown hair
and green eyes," says Jaime's mom.
"What's he wearing?" asks the guard.
"He's wearing a red shirt, blue jeans,
and a red baseball cap," says Jaime's mom.

A little later, Jaime remembers his mom.

"I'd better look for my mom," Jaime tells David.

Jaime goes back to the boys' department.

He does not see his mom anywhere! Jaime is scared.

Suddenly, Jaime hears someone calling his name. He sees his mom! He gives her a hug. They are happy to find each other. Jaime promises never to wander off again.

Let's Check!

A Think about the story. Answer the questions.

1. Where does Jaime go with his mom?
   a. store   b. school   c. library

2. How does Jaime feel when he can't find his mom?
   a. happy   b. excited   c. scared

3. How does Jaime's mom feel when Jaime is lost?
   a. excited   b. worried   c. happy

4. Where is Jaime when his mom finds him?
   a. toy department   b. parking lot   c. boys' department

5. How do Jaime and his mom feel at the end of the story?
   a. excited   b. worried   c. happy

B Write a complete sentence to answer each question.

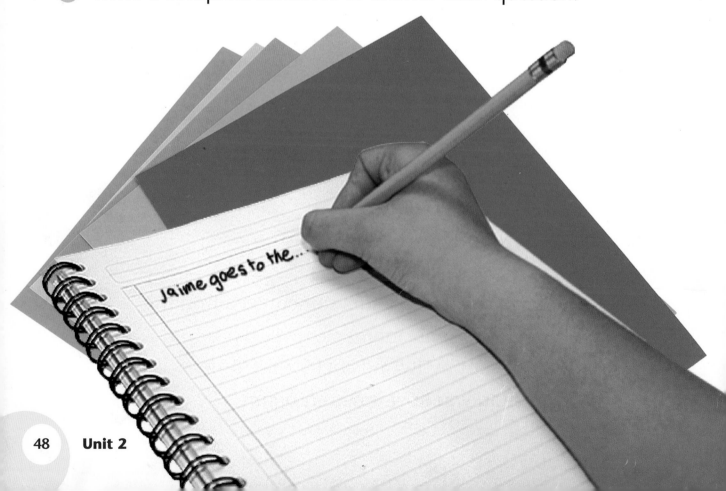

Let's Retell!

A Use the pictures to retell the story.

B Put the sentences in the correct order and write a summary of the story.

Jaime finds his mom.

Jaime and his mom go to a store.

Jaime's mom describes Jaime to the guard.

Jaime wanders off.

Let's Reflect!

▶ Discuss the questions.

1. Why did Jaime get lost?

2. How would you feel if you were lost?

3. What should you do if you were lost?

Spotlight on Language

Let's Connect!

▶ Listen and read, then point to David's mom.

Sir, can you help us?

I can't find my mom.

What does she look like?

She has long, blond hair and brown eyes.

What's she wearing?

She's wearing a blue skirt, a white blouse, and a pink sweater.

Is that your mother?

Let's Focus!

▶ Answer the questions.

blue	dress	green	long
shirt	shorts	blond	brown

1. What does the boy look like?

2. What is the boy wearing?

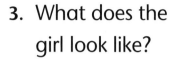

3. What does the girl look like?

4. What is the girl wearing?

Let's Apply!

▶ Pretend that you and a classmate are at the store, and one of you gets lost.

Student A: You are looking for one of your classmates at the store. Describe him or her to the security guard.

Student B: You are the security guard. Ask for a description of the lost classmate. Identify this student in your class.

Let's Connect!

A Look and read.

B Tell a friend what makes you feel scared, excited, nervous, angry, and lonely.

Let's Focus!

A Tell how you would feel in each of these situations.

> excited   angry   nervous   scared   lonely

1. You hear strange noises at night.

2. You have to talk in front of the class.

3. Your little sister draws in your favorite book.

4. None of your friends can come over to play.

5. You get a big box in the mail.

B Write a sentence about each situation.

Let's Apply!

▶ Play charades in a group.

1. Each student writes a different feeling on an index card.

2. Place the cards in a pile face down on a desk.

3. Take turns choosing a card.

4. Act out the feeling on the card.

5. The rest of your group guesses the feeling.

Let's Connect!

A Listen and point to what Jaime and David like and do not like.

Key Words

bikes
dolls
inline skates
puzzles
race cars
roller skates
scooter
skateboard
stuffed animals
toy

B Find out what a classmate does not like.

Let's Focus!

▶ Complete the sentences about the toys you like and do not like.

1. I like _____ and _____.

2. I do not like _____ or _____.

3. I like _____, but I do not like _____.

4. My favorite toy is _____.

Let's Apply!

A Use the questions to ask a partner about his or her toys.

1. What is your favorite toy?

2. What is your favorite game?

3. Do you like to ride a bike?

4. What toys don't you like?

B Write a report about your interview.

Interview

Alicia's favorite toy is a doll. Her favorite game is hide and seek. She likes to ride a bike, but she does not like roller skates.

An Invitation

You Are Invited!

What: A sleepover

When: Saturday, March 3, 2008 at 7:00 PM

Where: Ray Smith's house

       1542 Oak Street

       Rossmoor, CA 76534

RSVP: (306) 456-9876

Bring your sleeping bag, pillow, pajamas, and snacks to share!

Ray Smith
1542 Oak Street
Rossmoor, CA 76534

Jaime Garcia
1455 Elm Street
Rossmoor, CA 76534

▶ Answer the questions.

1. For what kind of event is the invitation?

2. How do you know *when* to go?

3. How do you know *where* to go?

4. Why is there a phone number?

Writing an Invitation

We use invitations to invite people to parties or special events. Invitations should include:

What: the kind of activity or event

When: the date and time of the event

Where: the location of the event

RSVP: The phone number you should call to say whether or not you are able to attend.

Other important information about what to bring or what to wear to the event.

A Write an invitation to a friend for a play date. Decorate your invitation.

B Use this checklist to make sure you included all the information.

Checklist
- ☐ What
- ☐ When
- ☐ Where
- ☐ RSVP
- ☐ Other Information

Come to Play !!

What: Come to play

When: Friday, after school

Where: Nancy's house

RSVP: (306) 457-4779

Ask for permission.

Capital Letters and Commas

Always capitalize the names of people and places:

People	**R**ay **S**mith
Streets	**O**ak **S**treet
Cities	**R**ossmoor
States	**C**alifornia

Always capitalize abbreviations:

California **CA**

Use commas to separate city and state:

Rossmoor**,** CA

Ray Smith
1542 Oak Street
Rossmoor, CA 76534

▶ Rewrite the names and addresses correctly in your notebook.

joe martin
4567 main street
austin tx 65473

VIA AIR MAIL   PAR AVION

sandy kent
1246 lemon avenue
miami fl 84950

Number Places

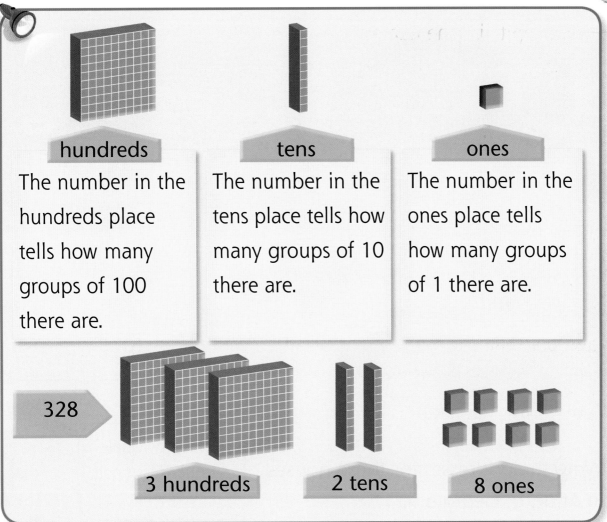

hundreds	tens	ones
The number in the hundreds place tells how many groups of 100 there are.	The number in the tens place tells how many groups of 10 there are.	The number in the ones place tells how many groups of 1 there are.

328

3 hundreds   2 tens   8 ones

▶ How many hundreds, tens, and ones are there?

1. Jan has 163 buttons.

   _____ hundreds _____ tens _____ ones

2. Rick has 215 marbles.

   _____ hundreds _____ tens _____ ones

3. Bob has 452 pennies.

   _____ hundreds _____ tens _____ ones

Writing Addresses

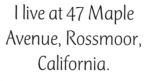

A Write the addresses for these houses in Atlanta, Georgia.

1. the red house

2. the orange house

3. the yellow house

4. the brown house

B Draw your house or apartment on your street.

C Write your address and phone number.

D Show your drawing to the class.

Where do you live?

I live at 47 Maple Avenue, Rossmoor, California.

The Five Senses

see

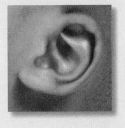
hear

smell

touch

taste

A Describe how the children are using their senses.

B Discuss the questions with your classmates.

1. How would you feel if you could not smell?

2. How would you feel if you could not feel what you touched?

3. Would you like your food if you could not taste?

Sing Along

A Listen to the song.

If You're Happy
And You Know It

If you're happy and you know it,
clap your hands.
If you're happy and you know it,
clap your hands.
If you're happy and you know it,
Then your face will really show it.
If you're happy and you know it,
clap your hands.

Hurray!

Music

B Sing the song again. Use the actions in the box.

stomp your feet   shout hurray

Painting with Dots

GEORGES SEURAT

Georges Seurat was a French painter. He was known for a style of painting called pointillism. He used tiny dots to create his images. Here is one of his famous paintings.

Ⓐ Answer the questions.

1. What are the colors in the painting?

2. Why is this style called pointillism?

3. What are the people in the painting doing?

4. What are they wearing?

Ⓑ Draw a picture of you and your friends having fun at the park.

Impressions

Staying Safe

In the United States, children often invite their friends to their homes. Parents usually let their children go places with their friends and their friends' parents. It is important to stay safe while you are with your friends.

Safety Tips

1. Never talk to strangers.
2. Never go anywhere with people you don't know.
3. Learn your address and phone number.
4. Pay attention to your surroundings.
5. Always make sure your parents know where you are.
6. In an emergency, call 911 or ask a police officer for help.
7. If you get lost in a busy place, stay where you are.

▶ Read the safety tips. Then, answer the questions about your country of origin.

1. What did you do to stay safe?

2. What number could you call in an emergency?

3. Who could you ask for help if you got lost?

All about Me Poster

▶ Create a poster about yourself.

Steps

1. Glue a photograph of yourself on a sheet of paper.

2. Write sentences about yourself. Include the following information:
   - name
   - age
   - address
   - where you come from
   - what you look like
   - what you like
   - what you don't like
   - what makes you feel happy
   - your favorite toy
   - your favorite color

3. Decorate your poster.

Supplies

- construction paper
- photograph of yourself
- glue
- markers

My name is Laura. I am seven years old.

My address is 370 Park Street, Weston, Florida.

I come from Spain. I have brown hair and blue eyes.

I like swimming. I don't like candy. Friends make me feel happy.

My favorite toy is my teddy bear. My favorite color is blue.

Unit 3 Home and Family

In my house down by the sea,
I live with my family.
My grandma and my grandpa Li
Don't live very near the sea.
They travel far just to see
My mom, dad, sister, and me.

I will learn to talk about ...

▸ family members

▸ rooms in a house

▸ chores

▸ feelings

Spotlight on Reading

Key Words

family

baby

crib

blanket

hospital

Let's Predict!

▶ Answer the questions.

1. What will the story be about?

2. What does the title of the story tell you?

3. What clues do the Key Words provide to what might happen in the story?

4. How do you think things will be when the new baby arrives?

OUR NEW BABY

by Tatiana Sildus

illustrated by Marcela Lescarboura

Jack peeks into the nursery. Dad is putting
the crib together.

"Can we go play baseball?" Jack asks.

"Not now," Dad says. "We're getting ready
for the baby."

Jack walks into the living room. Mom is knitting a pink blanket.

"Can we work on my rock collection?" Jack asks.

"Not now," Mom says. "We're getting ready for the baby."

Jack goes out to the backyard. He sits down
on the porch. There is no one to play with.
Everyone is getting ready for the baby. He is
not very happy about having a new sister.

The next day, Jack's grandma picks him
up from school.

"The baby is coming! Let's go to the
hospital," Grandma says. "Are you excited
to have a new sister?" she asks.

"Sure," Jack answers.

On the way to the hospital, Jack thinks
a lot. He doesn't feel excited. He feels scared.
He thinks no one will have time for him.
Everyone will be busy with the baby.

At the hospital, the family waits. Jack
watches his dad talk to Grandma. Sometimes
they look at him. He wonders what they
are talking about. He hopes his mom is OK.
Then the doctor calls Dad in.

They wait and wait and wait some more.
Finally, Dad comes back out.
"The baby is here!" says Dad.
Dad looks happy. Jack knows everything
is all right.

Jack goes in to see the baby. Baby Kate is so little! Mom hugs her close.

"Your sister is lucky to have such a smart brother," says Mom. "You can teach her many things. You will be my special helper."

"Don't worry, Jack," says Dad. "We will always have time for you. Do you want to go get some ice cream?"

"Sure!" Jack answers.

He is happy. Maybe having a new baby sister won't be so bad after all.

Let's Check!

A Answer the questions.

1. Who is the main character in the story?

      Kate   Jack   Dad

2. How does Jack feel at the beginning of the story about having a new sister?

     excited   scared   angry

3. How does Jack feel at the end of the story about having a new sister?

     worried   nervous   happy

B Discuss the questions.

1. Why are Jack's mom and dad busy at the beginning of the story?

2. Why does Jack feel scared?

3. Why does Jack feel better at the end of the story?

Let's Retell!

▶ Order the sentences and write a paragraph to retell the story.

Grandma picks Jack up from school.

Mom and Dad are too busy to play with Jack.

Jack is scared because he thinks no one will have time for him.

Baby Kate is born.

Jack and Dad go get ice cream.

Let's Reflect!

Good readers make predictions. A prediction is what you think will happen next.

▶ Read and discuss the questions.

1. What do you think will happen when baby Kate comes home from the hospital?

2. How will Jack help his mom and dad with the new baby?

3. How do you help your mom and dad around the house?

Spotlight on Language

Let's Connect!

A Listen and read the dialogue.

B Point to and name the people in Jack's family.

Let's Focus!

▶ Write sentences about Jack's family members.

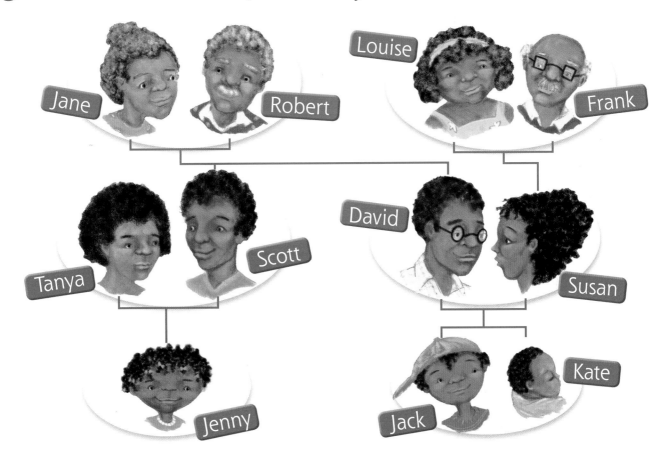

Let's Apply!

▶ Make a family tree. Draw the faces of your family members and write their names.

1. Draw your grandparents at the top.

2. Draw your parents, uncles, and aunts in the middle.

3. Draw yourself and your brothers, sisters, and cousins at the bottom.

4. Use lines to connect family members.

Let's Connect!

A Read about Jack's house.

I live in a house on Elm Street. There is a living room, a dining room, and a kitchen on the first floor. There are two bedrooms and a bathroom upstairs.

B Read about each room. Name the room.

There is a desk next to my bed.

There are towels on the shelf.

There are plates in the cupboard.

There are movies under the TV.

Let's Focus!

▶ Use the words in the chart to write sentences about Jack's house.

There is There are	a bed a desk a sink a couch a TV movies toothpaste a lamp pictures	in on under next to	the bedroom. the living room. the kitchen. the bathroom. the wall. the TV. the stove. the table. the drawer.

Let's Apply!

Ⓐ Copy and complete the chart with the furniture and objects found in each room in your house.

Living room	Kitchen	Bathroom	Bedroom

Ⓑ Write a paragraph describing your favorite room in your house.

Let's Connect!

A Listen and point to the people in the house.

Key Words

cooking dinner
drinking milk
dusting
feeding the baby
vacuuming the carpet
washing the dishes

B Say where the people are.

Let's Focus!

▶ Look at the picture of the house again. Answer the questions using the Key Words.

1. What is Mom doing?

2. What is the baby doing?

3. What is Dad doing?

4. What is Jack doing?

5. What is Grandma doing?

6. What is Grandpa doing?

Let's Apply!

▶ Imagine it is Saturday morning. Everyone is helping around your house.

1. Draw pictures of members of your family doing a chore.

2. Write a sentence about what each member is doing.

3. Describe your pictures to a classmate.

Spotlight on Content

A Friendly Letter

Date

June 10, 2007

Dear Jenny,

Salutation

Hello! I'm excited that you are coming to visit. My mom is getting a room ready for you. We are going to have so much fun. We can go swimming in the pool. We can also play video games. What else do you want to do? Are you nervous about flying on a plane alone? I can't wait for you to get here!

Body

Closing

Your cousin,

Signature

Jack

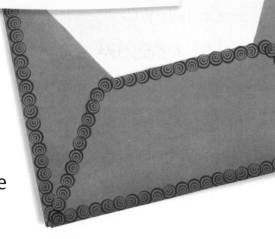

▶ Answer the questions about the letter.

1. What is the purpose of the letter?

2. Why include a date?

3. What word comes before the name in the salutation?

4. How do you know when a paragraph begins?

Writing a Friendly Letter

People write friendly letters to their friends and family for a variety of reasons. You can write to people to share news, to thank them, or even to invite them somewhere. Always remember to include:

- *The date:* Write the date at the upper right-hand side of the page. Separate the day and the year with a comma.
- *A salutation:* Write a comma after the name.
- *The body:* Indent the paragraphs.
- *A closing:* Center the closing and end with a comma.
- *Your signature:* Sign your name under the closing.

A Write a friendly letter to a relative. Answer the questions to help you get started.

1. Who are you writing to?

2. Why are you writing your letter?

3. What are some interesting things you can tell your relative about yourself?

4. What questions do you want to ask your relative?

B Use the checklist to check your letter.

Checklist
- ☐ Capitalization
- ☐ Order of Letter
- ☐ Punctuation
- ☐ Spelling

Using Commas

> Commas are used after a name in a salutation in a letter:
> *Dear Sara,*
> Commas are used to separate the day from the year:
> *June 10, 2007*
> Commas are used to set off items in a list:
> *I like to swim, ride my bike, and play soccer.*
> Commas are used to end a closing in a letter:
> *Your cousin,*
> *Juan*

A Rewrite each phrase or sentence using a comma.

1. September 25 2005

2. The baby needs a blanket a crib and a bottle.

3. Dear Dad

B Find the missing commas and other mistakes in the letter. Rewrite the letter correctly.

july 10 2007

dear mom

    I am having a great time with jack We swim in the pool ride bikes and play video games I miss you

                love

                jenny

Comparing Numbers

Higher numbers are *greater than* lower numbers.

Lower numbers are *less than* higher numbers.

Numbers that are the same are *equal*.

Use > to show *greater than*.

Use < to show *less than*.

Use = to show that two numbers are *equal*.

A Count each group of marbles. Tell which group is greater than or less than the other.

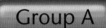 Group A

 Group B

B Copy and complete the number sentences with the correct symbol.

<   >   =

| 15 | 65 | | 78 | 78 | | 81 | 22 |

Family Responsibilities

Each member of the family has responsibilities. One or both parents work outside the home. They are responsible for earning money for housing, food, and other expenses. Children go to school. They are responsible for their grades and for being good citizens. At home, most families share household chores. Sometimes, family members have specific chores.

A Answer the questions about your family.

1. Who works outside your home?

2. Who goes to school in your family?

3. Who does the chores around your house?

4. Who does the shopping?

5. What would happen if no one cleaned your house?

B Create a weekly schedule with your home chores and responsibilities.

Bees

Bees are social insects. They live together in a hive. Each hive has "rooms" called cells. A queen bee, worker bees, and drones live in the hive. The queen bee decides where the hive will be built. The worker bees are her daughters. They all have chores, such as keeping the hive clean. They gather pollen and nectar from flowers. The worker bees also protect the hive.

A Answer the questions.

1. What is a hive made up of?

2. What is a chore of the queen bee?

3. How do you think the queen bee got her name?

4. What are two chores of worker bees?

5. How do you think worker bees got their name?

B Create a daily schedule of a worker bee's chores and responsibilities.

C Draw a worker bee doing its chores. Write a sentence to label your drawing.

Sing Along

A Listen to the song.

I Am Special!

I am special!
I am special!
Look at me.
You will see
Someone very special,
Someone very special.
It is me.
It is me.

B Sing the song. Use a friend's name and the words in the box.

is her him she he

Family Paintings

Carmen Lomas Garza

Carmen Lomas Garza is a famous Hispanic artist. Her family is very special to her, and she loves to paint pictures of family gatherings. Family gatherings are an important part of most cultures. Sometimes, families get together for a barbecue. Other times, families get together at a park, a home, or a restaurant. Wherever they go, families love to spend time together.

A Look at the two paintings and describe what you see to a partner.

B Tell your partner what your family does together.

C Paint a picture of your family sharing a special time.

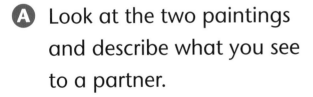

Impressions

Names

In the United States, many people have a first name, a middle name, and a last name. Some children are named after someone special, such as a relative or a famous person.

A Answer the questions.

1. How did your parents choose your name?

2. Are you named after someone special?

3. What does your name mean?

B Look at this chart of the most popular names in the United States. Find out if any students in your class have these names.

Boys' First Names	Girls' First Names	Last Names
Jacob	Emily	Smith
Michael	Emma	Johnson
Joshua	Madison	Williams
Ethan	Isabella	Jones
Mathew	Ava	Brown

C Talk about popular names in your country of origin.

Family Album

A Make a family album.

Steps

1. Use the cardstock paper for the front and the back of the album. Decorate the front and write the title *My Family Album*.

2. Use the construction paper for the pages. Glue two or three pictures on each page.

3. Write a caption for each picture.

4. Assemble the album and punch two holes along the left side.

5. Thread the ribbon through the holes and tie in a bow.

Supplies

- 2 sheets of cardstock paper
- construction paper
- pictures of your family (photos or drawings)
- glue
- hole punch
- ribbon

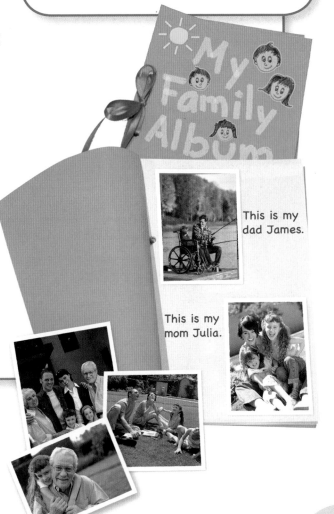

This is my dad James.

This is my mom Julia.

B Share your family album with your classmates.

Healthy Habits

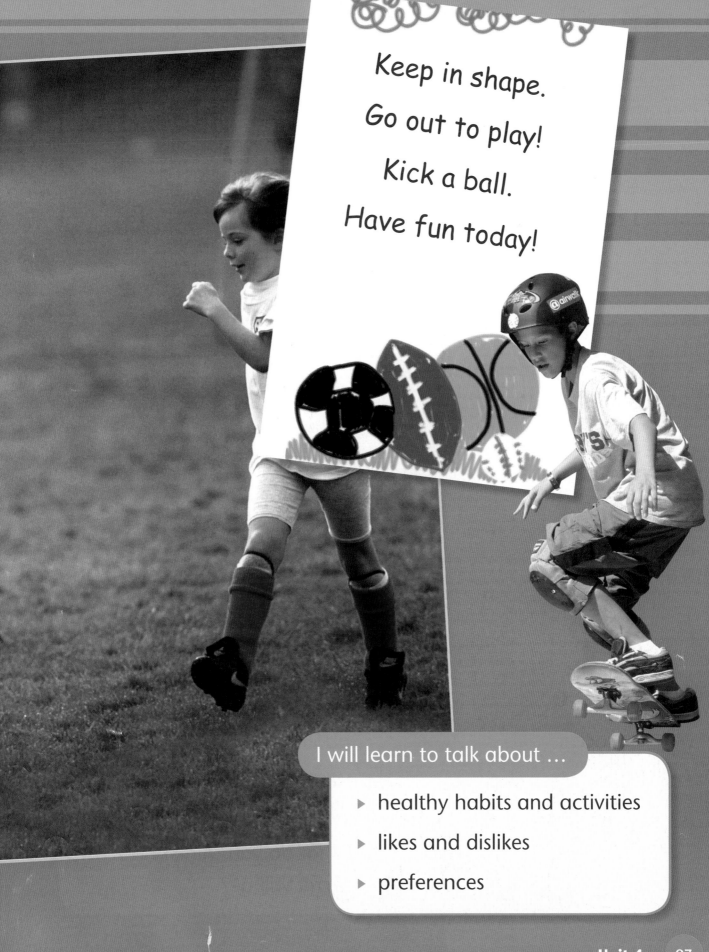

Keep in shape.
Go out to play!
Kick a ball.
Have fun today!

I will learn to talk about ...

▸ healthy habits and activities

▸ likes and dislikes

▸ preferences

Spotlight on Reading

coach

fruit

player

soccer

team

Let's Predict!

▶ Answer the questions.

1. What does the title tell you about the story?

2. What do you think the story will be about?

3. What do you think Ana's secret will be?

Ana's Secret

by Pablo Veramendi

Illustrated by Mariano Epelbaum

My older sister, Isabel, is great at sports! She's a wonderful soccer player. In the afternoons, she plays on a soccer team with some other girls.

I want to play on Isabel's team. So I
practice hard every day with my dad. He
teaches me how to kick the ball. He shows
me how to pass it. We don't tell Isabel that
I am practicing. We keep it a secret.

"You should practice hard every day,"
Dad says. "You should eat lots of fruit and
vegetables. And don't eat too much candy."
So I follow his rules.

One day Isabel comes home from soccer
practice. She's worried about the next game.
"Our best player can't come," Isabel tells
Dad. "What are we going to do?"

This is my big chance! The next day,
I go to the practice before the game.
"Can I play?" I ask the coach.
"Do you know how to play?" she asks.
She looks a little surprised.

The coach hands me a red shirt.
"Practice during the warm-up," she says.
"You'll play on the red team, Ana. Isabel will
play on the blue team."

The warm-up starts. I dribble the ball down the field. Isabel tries to block me. I run past her with the ball. I dribble the ball back very fast. I score a goal!

"Wow!" says Isabel. "That was a great move!"

"Ana can play," shouts the coach. "She's a good player!"

Soon the game starts. Our team plays hard. We win the game!

After the game, Isabel comes up to me.
She gives me a hug.

"Ana, you're a good player!" she says.
She looks excited. "We have another athlete in
the family! Now we can play together."

Let's Check!

▶ Answer the questions.

1. What is Ana's sister good at?

2. What does Ana do to get ready to play on Isabel's team?

3. Who helps Ana practice?

4. How does the story end?

Let's Retell!

A Rewrite the sentences in the correct order.

Ana scores a goal.

Ana practices soccer with her dad.

The team wins the game.

Ana plays well in the warm-up.

Ana asks the coach if she can play.

B Use the sentences as a guide to retell the story.

Let's Reflect!

A The children in the story enjoy soccer. Talk about a sport that you like and share why you enjoy it.

B Ana practices soccer and eats fruit and vegetables to stay healthy. Write a list of things you can do to exercise and stay healthy.

Spotlight on Language

Let's Connect!

A Read the chart that shows what Ana does during the week.

Activity	Always	Often	Sometimes	Never
eats fruit	X			
exercises		X		
stretches her muscles			X	
washes her hands		X		
gets plenty of rest	X			
eats lots of candy				X

B Work with a partner. Answer the questions.

1. How often does Ana eat vegetables?

2. How often does Ana exercise?

3. How often does Ana get plenty of rest?

4. How often does Ana eat candy?

Key Words

always
habit
never
often
sometimes

Let's Focus!

▶ Read and answer.

1. Isabel does her homework every afternoon. Does she do her homework always or sometimes?

2. Ana exercises three times a week. Does she do her exercises sometimes or never?

3. Isabel eats vegetables every day. Does she eat her vegetables always or often?

Words That Tell How Often

- *Always* means all the time.
- *Often* means most of the time.
- *Sometimes* means some of the time.
- *Never* means none of the time.

Let's Apply!

▶ Copy the chart. Check the habits you practice each day of the week.

Habit	Sun.	Mon.	Tue.	Wed.	Thur.	Fri.	Sat.
eat vegetables							
eat candy							
eat fruit							
exercise							

Let's Connect!

A Listen to the coach talk about healthy habits.

Key Words

habits
healthy
meal
rest
snack
water

B Answer the questions.

1. What things should the players do?

2. What things should the players not do?

Let's Focus!

A Say if you should or should not practice these habits.

1. skip meals

2. drink plenty of water

3. wear a helmet to ride a bicycle

4. eat lots of candy

B Write your sentences in your notebook.

Let's Apply!

▶ Play a memory game with a partner.

1. Write habits and activities that you should and should not do on 3″× 5″ index cards. Make two sets.

2. Mix the index cards. Place them face down in rows of five.

3. Turn over two cards at one time. Each time you turn over a card, say what you should or should not do.

4. If the cards match, keep the pair. The student with the most pairs wins.

Drink plenty of water.

Eat vegetables.

Eat a lot of candy.

Let's Connect!

▶ Listen and read about what Isabel likes, prefers, and does not like.

Let's Focus!

▶ Follow the directions.

1. Choose the foods you like, the foods you do not like, and the foods you prefer.

grapes   apples   soup   carrots

chicken   pizza   broccoli   fish

2. Write the foods you like, the foods you do not like, and the foods you prefer in the chart.

Like	Do Not Like	Prefer

3. Share your chart with a partner.

Let's Apply!

▶ Make a booklet about things you like, prefer, and do not like.

1. Fold and staple four sheets of paper.

2. Write a title for your booklet.

3. Write six sentences about foods you like, prefer, and do not like.

4. Illustrate your booklet.

5. Read your booklet to a friend.

I like ice cream cones.

Advertisements

▶ Read and answer the questions.

1. What is the purpose of the music advertisement?

2. What is the purpose of the drink advertisement?

3. What does the advertisement tell you about the student talent contest?

4. What does the advertisement tell you about the drink?

Writing an Advertisement

Authors or writers write for many purposes. One of them is to get people to do or buy something. This is called writing to persuade. Sometimes, a person writes an advertisement to persuade people to do something. An advertisement can also persuade people to buy the advertised item.

A Write an advertisement about a healthy snack you want people to buy.

1. Give the snack a name.

2. Draw a picture of the snack.

3. Write two sentences to persuade people to buy the snack.

B Write an advertisement about a movie you want people to see.

1. Give the movie a name.

2. Write what type of movie it is.

3. Draw a picture from a scene in the movie.

4. Write two sentences to persuade people to see the movie.

Using Adjectives

An adjective is a word that describes a person, place, or thing. Often, the adjective comes before the word it describes. Here are some examples of adjectives:

- To describe a person:
  Isabel is a *good* soccer player.
- To describe a place:
  The soccer field is *big*.
- To describe a thing:
  The *blue* shirt belongs to Isabel.

▶ Choose one of the adjectives to complete each circle of the word web.

pure   every   fresh   clean   healthy

1. Exercise _____ day.

3. Drink _____ water.

Healthy Activities

2. Eat _____ fruit.

4. Eat _____ snacks.

5. Wear _____ clothes.

118   Unit 4

Money

In the United States, dollars are used as currency. Many different combinations of coins make up a dollar. One dollar is made up of one hundred cents, or pennies. Twenty nickels equal one dollar. Ten dimes equal one dollar. And four quarters equal one dollar. Quarters, dimes, and nickels are coins that combine different groups of cents. One quarter is twenty-five cents, one dime is ten cents, and one nickel is five cents.

▶ Read the text and answer the questions.

Susan likes to visit the snack bar for a healthy snack. She has two quarters and five pennies.

1. How much money does Susan have in cents?

2. How many oranges can Susan buy with her money?

3. How much does one bottle of water cost?

Strawberries 50¢

Grapes 35¢

Oranges 25¢

Water 75¢

Cheese Crackers 90¢

Juice 85¢

Granola Bar 95¢

How Milk Is Produced

Milk is good for you! Do you know where milk comes from? It usually comes from cows. Today, dairy farmers use special machines to milk the cows. Most people buy milk in a store. The milk is sold in plastic bottles.

Long ago, dairy farmers milked cows by hand. This milk was sold in glass bottles. People didn't buy milk at a store. Instead, milk was delivered to your home by a milkman.

▶ Copy and complete the Venn diagram.

Milk Production

Today   Long Ago

Force

In order to move something, you must give it a push or a pull.

A push is when you move something away from you.

A pull is when you move something toward you.

The harder you push or pull, the faster the object will move. How hard you push or pull is called "force."

A Look at each picture and tell whether the person is pushing or pulling the object.

B Answer the questions.

1. What happens when you push a ball hard?

2. What happens when you push a ball gently?

C Write your results in your notebook.

Sing Along

A Listen to the song.

The children in the class will
Stretch their arms, stretch their arms, stretch their arms.
The children in the class will stretch their arms
'Cause they are healthy kids!

The children in the class will
Bend their legs, bend their legs, bend their legs.
The children in the class will bend their legs
'Cause they are healthy kids!

B Sing the song.

C Sing the song again. Use the healthy habits in the box.

jump up high	squat down low
run in place	walk in place

Making a Collage

A collage is an artwork of different materials and objects glued onto a sheet of paper. The materials can be arranged in any way on the paper. Usually the images are related by topic.

Steps

1. Look through the magazines and cut out pictures that show people playing your favorite sports.

2. Glue the pictures onto a large sheet of butcher paper.

3. Glue on sports materials such as game schedules or tickets.

4. Make a title for your collage.

5. Display your collage in the classroom.

6. Discuss your favorite sport or sports with your classmates.

Supplies

- large sheet of butcher paper
- sports-related magazines
- tickets to sports events, game schedules, etc.
- scissors
- glue

Impressions

Playtime

Playtime is a great way to stay healthy and meet new friends. In the United States, children like to play games of tag, jump rope, and hopscotch during playtime. What games do you like to play?

▶ Follow the instructions.

1. Talk about popular playtime activities in your country of origin.

2. Tell your partner how to play a game from your country of origin.

3. Play the game with your classmates.

HEALTH Fair

▶ In groups of three or four, make an advertisement for a classroom health fair.

Steps

1. Decide on a persuasive sentence to invite other students to the fair. Write it at the top of the construction paper.

2. Write another sentence about the health fair activities.

3. Draw a picture showing your classmates doing these activities.

4. Include the date, time, and location of the health fair.

5. Display your advertisement in the school hallway.

Supplies

- construction paper
- crayons or markers

Come to Our Health Fair!
Play fun games for health.
September 15, 1:00 PM
Mr. Smith's Grade 2 Classroom

Unit 5 Community

There is a place you can call home, where you can meet friendly people like doctors, bus drivers, and mail carriers. There are buildings, houses, schools, and grocery stores. There are streets with cars and buses. There are also fun places like parks and museums! What is it?

I will learn to talk about ...

▸ community places

▸ community workers

▸ locations

▸ directions

Key Words

bus driver

dumpster

grocer

poster

mail carrier

Let's Predict!

▷ Answer the questions.

1. What is the story about?

2. Where will the story take place?

3. What will happen to the dog?

The Mystery of the Missing Dog

by Sarah Fash
Illustrated by Mima Castro

Jake and Max are best friends. Max does just about everything Jake does. Max would even go to school with Jake, but everyone knows dogs aren't allowed at school.

One morning when Jake woke up,
something didn't feel right. Jake looked
around. He couldn't find Max.
"Max! Max!" Jake called out. But Max
was nowhere to be found.

Jake ran into the kitchen.
"Mom! I can't find Max anywhere!"
Jake's mom looked up from the newspaper.
"I'm sure he's here somewhere, Jake. Why don't you get dressed and go look outside?"

After getting dressed, Jake ran outside.
Max wasn't there! Where could Max be?
It was time to go to school.

"Jake!" his mom called out. "You'll miss
the bus. Don't worry! Your dad and I will
look for Max while you're gone."

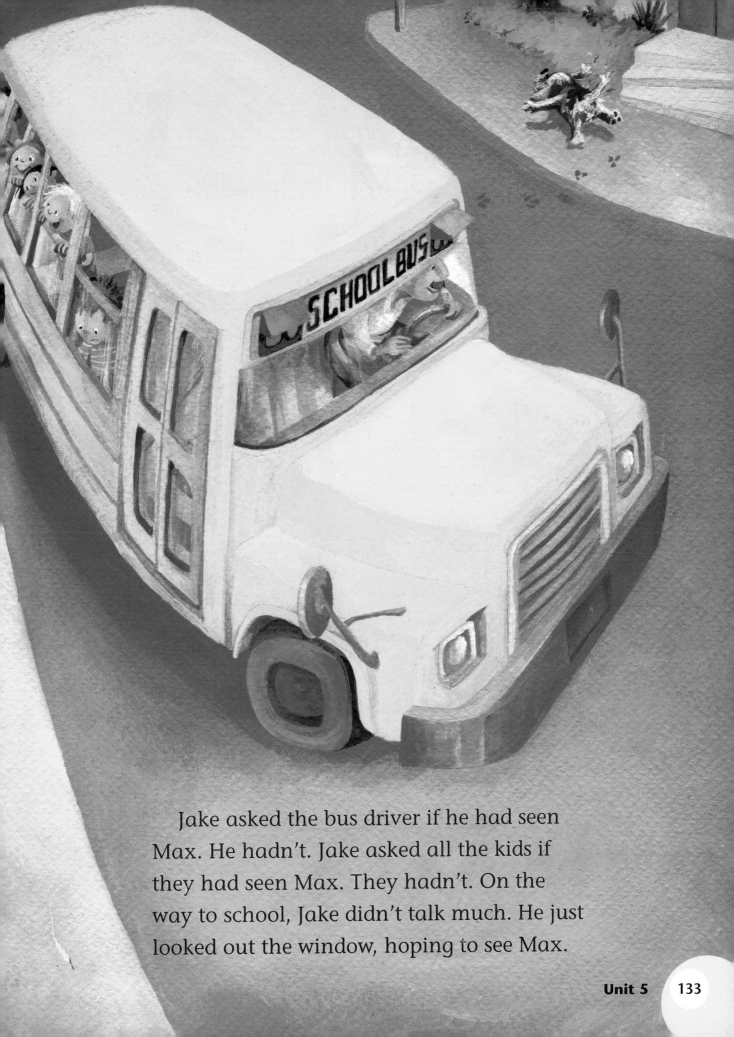

Jake asked the bus driver if he had seen
Max. He hadn't. Jake asked all the kids if
they had seen Max. They hadn't. On the
way to school, Jake didn't talk much. He just
looked out the window, hoping to see Max.

Jake ran into his house after school.
"Mom!" he called. "Did you find him?"
"Sorry, Jake!" his mom answered. "I can't
find him anywhere. I made these posters.
Let's go see if we can find him."

Jake and his mom walked around town, putting up posters. They saw the mail carrier. "Have you seen this dog?" Jake asked. "Sorry! I saw a little brown dog a few minutes ago. But I haven't seen that dog."

Later, they passed the grocery store.

"Have you seen this dog?" Jake asked
the grocer.

"I saw him over by the dumpster," said
the grocer.

Jake ran over to the dumpster.

"Max!" he shouted. "How in the world did you get so dirty? And how did you get out of the house?"

Jake's mom started to laugh.

"Max!" she said. "Let's go home. You need a good bath!"

Let's Check!

A Write the sentences in the order they happened in the story.

Jake found Max near the dumpster.

Jake and his mom asked the mail carrier if she had seen Max.

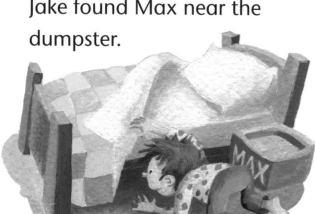

Jake couldn't find Max anywhere.

Jake looked for Max outside.

B Who is the main character in the story?

C What steps did Jake take to find Max?

Let's Summarize!

▶ Follow the directions.

1. Name the characters in the story.

2. Name the places where Jake looked for Max.

3. Use the character names and the places to summarize the story.

Let's Reflect!

Ⓐ Think about a time when you lost something special.

1. What was it?

2. How did you feel when you lost it?

3. Did you find it? Where did you find it?

4. How did you feel when you found it?

Ⓑ Write about your experience.

Ⓒ Share your writing with a classmate.

Spotlight on Language

Let's Connect!

A Read Jake's report about a field trip he took with his class.

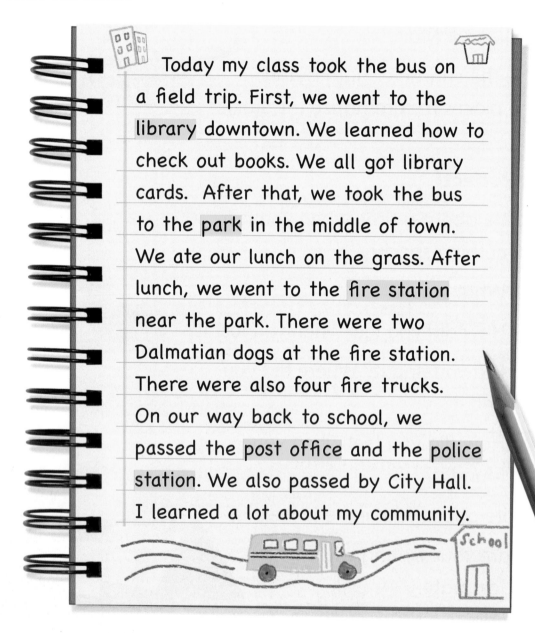

Today my class took the bus on a field trip. First, we went to the library downtown. We learned how to check out books. We all got library cards. After that, we took the bus to the park in the middle of town. We ate our lunch on the grass. After lunch, we went to the fire station near the park. There were two Dalmatian dogs at the fire station. There were also four fire trucks. On our way back to school, we passed the post office and the police station. We also passed by City Hall. I learned a lot about my community.

B Tell where the class went first, next, and last.

Let's Focus!

▶ Match the item with the community location.

Let's Apply!

Ⓐ Think about a time when you visited two of the places in the pictures.

Ⓑ Write three or four sentences about what you saw and did there.

school

park

library

grocery store

Let's Connect!

A Listen and read about the community workers Jake met on his field trip.

> I am the mayor. I work at City Hall. I manage the city where people live. I am a community leader.

> I am a firefighter. I work at the fire station. I put out fires and rescue people and animals in danger.

> I am a police officer. I work at the police station. I help keep the city safe.

> I am a librarian. I work at the library. I help people find and check out books.

> I am a mail carrier. I work at the post office. I deliver the mail.

B Say what each community worker does.

Let's Focus!

A Match the worker with the location.

B Write what the workers do to help the community.

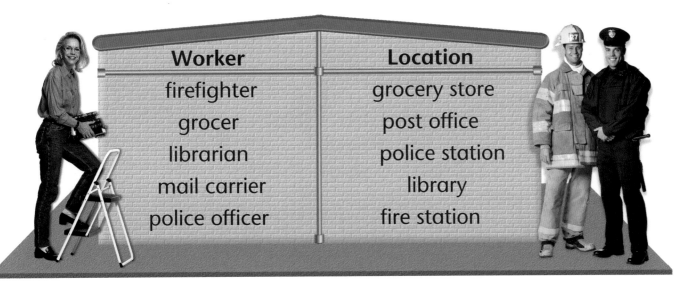

Worker	Location
firefighter	grocery store
grocer	post office
librarian	police station
mail carrier	library
police officer	fire station

Let's Apply!

grocery store   post office   grocer
police station   firefighter
fire station   mail carrier
library   librarian
City Hall   mayor   police officer
manages the city

A Mix and match community workers.

1. Make separate sets of cards that tell about community workers: name of workers, where they work, and what they do.

2. Place the cards face down in three separate groups.

3. Flip over one card from each group.

4. If the cards match, keep the cards. That's your community worker!

5. If the cards are not a match, turn them back over.

B Write a paragraph about the community worker described on your matching cards.

Let's Connect!

▶ Listen and point to the locations on the map.

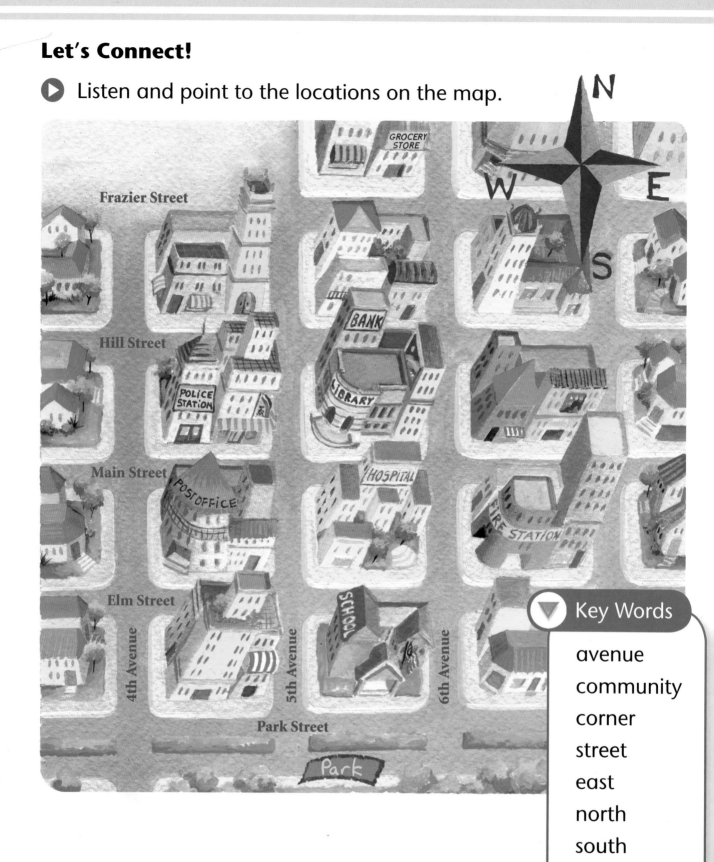

Key Words

avenue

community

corner

street

east

north

south

west

Let's Focus!

A Follow the directions. Write your answers in your notebook.

1. Start at the bank. Go west one block. What avenue are you on now?

2. Start at the library. Go south one block. Where are you now? What building is on this corner?

3. Start at the corner of 6th Avenue and Park Street. Go north one block. Where are you now? What building is on this corner?

B Answer the questions in your notebook.

1. What is on the corner of Elm Street and 4th Avenue?

2. What is on the corner of Main Street and 5th Avenue?

3. What is on the corner of Frazier Street and 6th Avenue?

Let's Apply!

A Tell how to get from your home to these locations:
1. school
2. park
3. grocery store

B Write the directions.

A Newspaper Article

The News

Local Students Lend a Hand

Brentwood CA

Students from Tracy Elementary School met this weekend to clean up the neighborhood after last week's storms. Although most of the students do not live in the area, they still wanted to help.

"We wanted to help our neighbors," said fourth grader, Joe Martin.

According to their principal, Ms. Jones, students expressed a desire to help after watching the storms on the news. They met on Saturday and spent the day picking up trash.

"It was hard work," reported Misty Cruz, a sixth grader. "But it was worth it."

▶ Answer the questions.

1. *Who* is the article mostly about?

2. *Where* do the students go to school?

3. *What* did the students do?

4. *Why* is it important to help the community?

Writing a Newspaper Article

A newspaper article informs you about many things. It can tell you about a person or event in your community. *Who*, *What*, *Where*, *When*, and *Why* are five important details of any newspaper article.

A Copy and complete the chart with information about something exciting that happened in your school or community.

Who	What	Where	When	Why

B Write a newspaper article about what happened using the information in your chart.

C Share your article with the class.

D Put your articles together to create a class newspaper.

Synonyms and Antonyms

A synonym is a word that has the same meaning as another word.

An antonym is a word that has the opposite meaning of another word.

hot

cold

▶ Copy the chart and write each pair of words in the correct column.

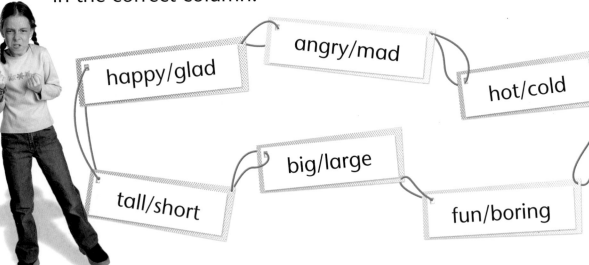

happy/glad

angry/mad

hot/cold

big/large

tall/short

fun/boring

antonyms	synonyms

Graphs

A graph is a chart that helps you see the relationship between two or more things. It can help you see how two or more things are the same or different. A graph can also help you see how things change over time.

A Look at the bar graph. Answer the questions.

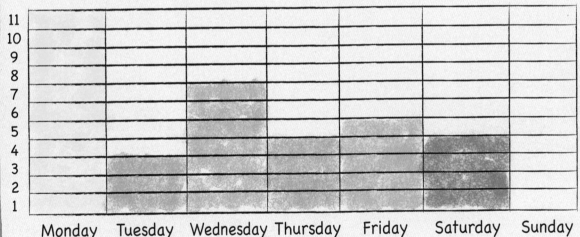

Mindy used a bar graph to keep track of her family's mail for one week. Each day, she counted how many letters came in the mail.

1. How many letters did the family receive on Monday?

2. On what day did the family receive the least mail?

3. On what day did the family receive the most mail?

4. What would be a good title for this graph?

B Make your own bar graph. List the number of chores you do each day of the week.

Urban, Suburban, and Rural Areas

In urban areas, there are many factories. A factory is a building where things are made. Many different things are made in factories, including cars and planes.

Suburban areas often have many homes and shopping malls. People like to live in suburban areas because of the space and convenience. Usually, families need a car to live in this area.

In rural areas, there are farms of different sizes. Many things are grown on farms, like fruits and vegetables. Animals, like chickens and cattle, are also raised on farms.

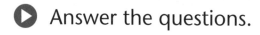

▶ Answer the questions.

1. What are three things that come from farms?

2. In what kind of area would you find a factory?

3. Why do people like to live in suburban areas?

4. Do you live in an urban, a rural, or a suburban area? Describe the area.

Natural Resources

Earth provides many natural resources that we use every day. Soil, trees, oil, and water are examples of natural resources.

Soil provides nutrients for plants to grow. We then eat some of these plants.

Trees and plants also provide wood and fiber for clothing. Many homes and buildings are made from wood. Many clothes are made of cotton fiber. Your favorite shirt is probably made from cotton.

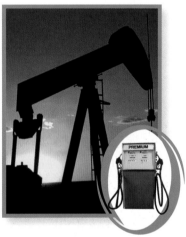

A Make a list of things that come from these natural resources:

1. cotton

2. wood

3. oil

B Discuss why these resources are important.

Music

A Listen to the song.

Community Helper Song

The doctor heals the sick.
The doctor heals the sick.
She works inside the hospital.
The doctor heals the sick.

The grocer sells the food.
The grocer sells the food.
He works inside the grocery store.
The grocer sells the food.

The officer keeps us safe.
The officer keeps us safe.
She works inside the station.
The officer keeps us safe.

B Sing the song.

C Make up verses to the song using this list.

teacher/school   secretary/office
bus driver/bus

Potted Plant Stand

Wood comes from trees. It is used to make many things we use, such as doors, tables, toys, and much more. Popsicle sticks are also made from wood. You can use popsicle sticks to make a stand for a potted plant.

▶ Make a stand for a potted plant.

Steps

1. Cut a 5" x 5" cardboard square.

2. Glue several sticks next to each other to cover the cardboard square.

3. Glue a second layer of sticks on top of the first layer.

4. Stack the sticks high enough to support a small flower pot.

5. Let the stand dry overnight.

6. Take the stand home to paint.

Supplies

- several popsicle sticks
- scissors
- 5" x 5" cardboard
- glue

Getting Around

In many countries, there are different ways to get from one place to another. Look at the pictures and read about kinds of transportation people use to move around their communities in the United States.

A train has several cars connected to each other. It travels on a track. In the city, many people take trains to get around very quickly!

A car travels on paved roads. People who live in the suburbs need cars to get from one place to another.

A public bus carries many passengers at once. It travels on paved roads. People use the bus to get around town without the need of a car.

A Discuss the different kinds of transportation people use to get around in your country of origin.

B Tell how these kinds of transportation are the same or different from the ones in the community where you live.

C Tell which is your favorite kind of transportation and why.

A Make a map of your community.

Steps

1. Draw a map of your community.

2. Label the streets.

3. Label the places.

Supplies

- construction paper
- markers and crayons

B Talk about your community.

1. Point to and talk about the places you have visited.

2. Point to the place where you would like to work. Explain the work that you would do.

Unit 6 My World

It is large and almost round.
The colors are blue
and brown.
There are also swirls of white.
It even glows at night.
What a wonderful sight!
What is it?

I will learn to talk about ...

▸ physical features of Earth

▸ climate and weather

▸ seasons

Spotlight on Reading

Key Words

planet

desert

mountain

bodies of water

forest

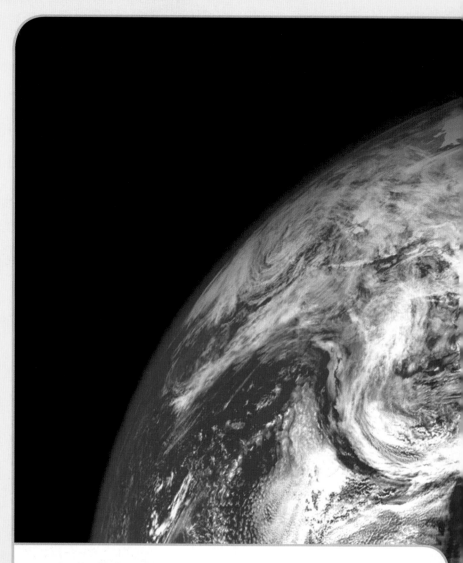

Let's Predict!

▶ Answer the questions.

1. What does the title tell you about the passage?

2. Why do you think Earth is an amazing place?

3. What do you think you will learn about Earth?

Our Amazing Earth!

by Sarah Fash

Earth is an amazing planet! The surface of Earth is made of land and water. The land and the water form many different shapes.

A mountain is a very high piece of land. Mount Everest is the tallest mountain in the world. It is in Asia. Most of Mount Everest is always covered with snow.

A volcano is a mountain that can erupt. When the volcano erupts, very hot lava and steam come out of it. Then, the lava cools and hardens into rock.

Oceans are large bodies of water. All oceans have salt water. Earth has five oceans. They are the Atlantic Ocean, the Pacific Ocean, the Indian Ocean, the Southern Ocean, and the Arctic Ocean.

A river is a large, flowing body of water.
The longest river in the world is the Nile.
The Nile River is in Africa. It floods every
summer because of rain.

Deserts are very dry areas. The largest
desert in the world is the Sahara. It is in
Africa. There is not much water in a desert.
Still, many kinds of plants and animals
live there.

Lakes are bodies of water surrounded by land. Most lakes have freshwater. The Great Lakes are five large lakes in North America.

Forests are places with lots of trees and plants. There are different kinds of forests. Tropical forests are near the equator. They have a rainy season and a dry season.

Our Earth is a beautiful place. There are many kinds of landforms. There are also many bodies of water. Both make up the surface of Earth.

Let's Check!

A Name each landform and body of water.

B Answer the questions with complete sentences.

1. What are two things you learned from the passage?

2. Which landform is higher than all the rest?

3. What place is hot and dry?

4. How many oceans are there? What are their names?

Let's Summarize!

▶ Think about the passage. Answer the questions.

1. What is the main idea of the passage?

2. How does the author support the main idea?

Let's Reflect!

Ⓐ Earth is an amazing place. Talk about the things you find amazing about Earth.

Ⓑ Write a list of places from the passage that you would like to visit.

Ⓒ Draw a picture of your favorite place on Earth.

Spotlight on Language

Let's Connect!

A Listen to the information about Mount Everest and the Sahara Desert.

B Discuss the weather and climate on Mount Everest and in the Sahara Desert.

Key Words

calm
clear
climate
cloudy
cold
dry
hot
rainy
snowy
weather
windy

Let's Focus!

A Describe the weather in each picture.

B Answer the questions about the weather in your neighborhood.

1. What is the weather like today?

2. What was the weather like yesterday?

3. What do you think the weather will be like tomorrow?

Let's Apply!

A Check your local weather forecast for the week.

B Draw a picture and write a sentence to describe the weather for each day of the week.

Let's Connect!

A Listen and read about the seasons.

Summer

Summer is a time for fun! It is the hottest season of the year. People go swimming to stay cool. Daylight lasts longer than in any other season.

Fall

In fall, the leaves on the trees change from green to orange, yellow, red, or brown. The days get shorter and shorter. Some birds fly south.

Winter

Winter is the coldest of the four seasons. Some birds fly south, to a warmer climate. In many areas, there is a lot of snow, and children make snowmen.

Spring

Spring is a time for new life. Leaves grow back on the trees. Flowers bloom. The days begin to get warmer and longer. It is almost time for summer again!

B Draw and label each season.

C Write a sentence describing what happens in each season.

Let's Focus!

▶ Answer each question with a complete sentence.

1. Which season is the hottest?

2. Is it colder in fall or in summer?

3. Is it warmer in spring or in winter?

Fall

Let's Apply!

Ⓐ Make a seasons poster.

1. Divide a sheet of paper into four sections and label them with the names of the seasons.

2. Draw an activity that you can do in each season.

Ⓑ Describe what you can do and cannot do in each season.

Ⓒ Write one sentence to describe each season.

Winter

Summer

Spring

Let's Connect!

▶ Read the riddles. Try to guess the answer.

It is filled with freshwater and is completely surrounded by land. Fish and plants live in it. It may have small waves. Many people love to water-ski on it. What is it?

It is hot and dry. It is made of sand. The plants that grow there do not need a lot of water. Some people like to ride camels in it. What is it?

It is huge and full of salt water. Many different kinds of plants and animals live in it. People love to surf and sail on it. Near the shore, people play in the sand and make sandcastles. What is it?

It is big and high. It is made of soil or rock. In some places the surface may be smooth, and in other places it may be rough. Many people like to climb it. What is it?

▼ Key Words

desert
lake
mountain
ocean

Let's Focus!

▶ Choose the word that completes the sentence.

1. The desert (is / are) a very dry area.

2. Some mountains (has / have) a smooth surface.

3. Many fish (live / lives) in lakes.

4. People (swim / swims) in the ocean.

Let's Apply!

▶ Use a Venn diagram to compare and contrast lakes and oceans.

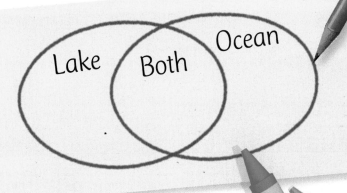

Language Arts

Expository Writing

The Effects Of Weather

Weather affects landforms in many ways. Wind and rain break off pieces of rock from the mountains. This action is called *erosion*. These pieces of rock are carried to another place by wind and rain.

Erosion causes the shape of mountains to change. Wind also blows sand in the desert and on beaches. This changes the shape of the land. Sometimes, rain can also cause a landslide.

▶ Read the text and answer the questions.

1. What does the title tell you about the reading?

2. What is the author trying to describe or explain?

Writing an Expository Paragraph

Expository writing explains or describes something. It gives the reader information about a topic. Expository writing has a title, a topic sentence, and facts about what is being explained or described. The topic sentence is usually the first sentence.

▶ Write an expository paragraph.

1. Pick a physical feature of Earth: a mountain, a lake, a forest, an ocean, a desert, or a river.

2. Read about the feature you have chosen.

3. Write down facts that you learn.

4. Write a paragraph that describes the feature you have chosen. Remember to include a title, a topic sentence, and facts.

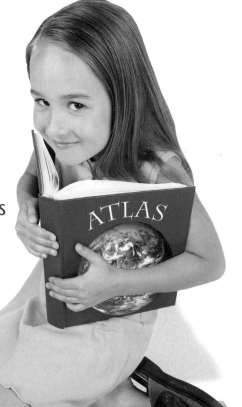

Regular Plurals

Sometimes, we write about only one person, place, or thing. *There is one mountain.*

Other times, we write about more than one person, place, or thing. *There are several mountains.*

When writing about more than one of something, we usually add an s to the end of the noun.

▶ Follow the directions.

1. Draw more than one of each object.

2. Write the name of the object.

3. Add an *s* at the end of the word to show that there is more than one.

4. Write a sentence using each plural word.

Telling Time

To tell time, first, look at the hour hand, and then the minute hand.

The numbers on a clock show the hour.

There are five minutes between each of the big numbers on a clock.

When writing the time, write the hour first, then a colon, then the minutes.

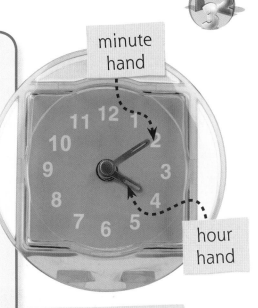

minute hand

hour hand

The time on this clock is 4:10.

A Tell the time on each clock.

B Copy the clocks. Draw the hour and the minute hand on each clock.

2:30   6:00   12:00   8:00

Caring for Our Earth

There are many ways to take care of Earth. In this community, citizens are having a clean-up day at the park. Everyone is helping. Some people are picking up trash. Others are recycling bottles and cans. In another area of the park, a girl is planting a tree.

A Describe how the people are taking care of Earth.

B Make a list of ways you can take care of Earth. Share the list with your classmates.

Fossils

Fossils are the remains of an animal or plant that lived a long time ago. A fossil forms when an animal or plant dies and is buried under layers of mud or sand. The hard parts of the animal or plant are replaced with minerals. The minerals form the fossil. The fossil is as hard as a rock.

A Make a fossil.

Supplies

clay or play dough

tagboard

Steps

1. Mix the clay or play dough.

2. Flatten a ball of clay or dough on a square piece of tagboard.

3. Make an imprint of your hand, a leaf, a shell, or other object.

4. Let the clay or dough dry.

5. Remove the object from the clay or dough.

B Describe your fossil to your classmates.

C Discuss how fossils are useful to people.

Sing Along

A Listen to the song.

🎵 Here We Go 'round the Planet Earth

Here we go 'round the planet Earth,
the planet Earth, the planet Earth.
Here we go 'round the planet Earth
to see what we can see.

The mountains are tall on planet Earth,
on planet Earth, on planet Earth.
The mountains are tall on planet Earth.
They reach up to the sky.

The oceans are deep on planet Earth,
on planet Earth, on planet Earth.
The oceans are deep on planet Earth
and filled with plants and fish.

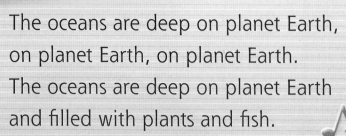

B Sing the song. Then, change the words of the song to include other features of Earth.

Art

Landscape Painting

Georgia O'Keefe

Georgia O'Keefe was a famous American painter. She was born in Wisconsin in 1887. She studied art for many years. One summer she visited New Mexico and felt inspired by the landscape. Every year she went back to New Mexico to paint. Her desert landscape paintings of New Mexico made her famous all over the world.

A Answer the questions.

1. What landscape did the artist paint?

2. What do you like about the painting?

B Paint a landscape scene.

Steps

1. Choose a place to paint, such as the beach, the mountains, or the desert.

2. Decide which colors you will need.

3. Draw your scene using a pencil.

4. Then, paint your scene.

Supplies

- white construction paper
- pencil
- crayons or colored pencils
- nature magazine for ideas

Tracing Our Roots

Except for Native Americans, everyone in the United States can trace their roots to other parts of the world. For example, some of our families came from Asia, and some came from Latin America. The country you and your family came from is an important part of who you are today.

A Point to the part of the world map that shows where your family came from.

B Discuss why the country you and your family came from is an important part of who you are today.

Project

My Favorite Place in the United States

A Write an expository paragraph about a physical feature in the United States.

Supplies

- an atlas, an encyclopedia, and/or the Internet

Steps

1. Choose your favorite landform or body of water.

2. Read information about the landform or body of water you have chosen.

3. Write down the facts. Remember to include:
   a. location
   b. climate and seasons
   c. plants
   d. animals

4. Write a paragraph that describes the feature you have chosen.

B Read your paragraph to your class.

Unit 7 Animals

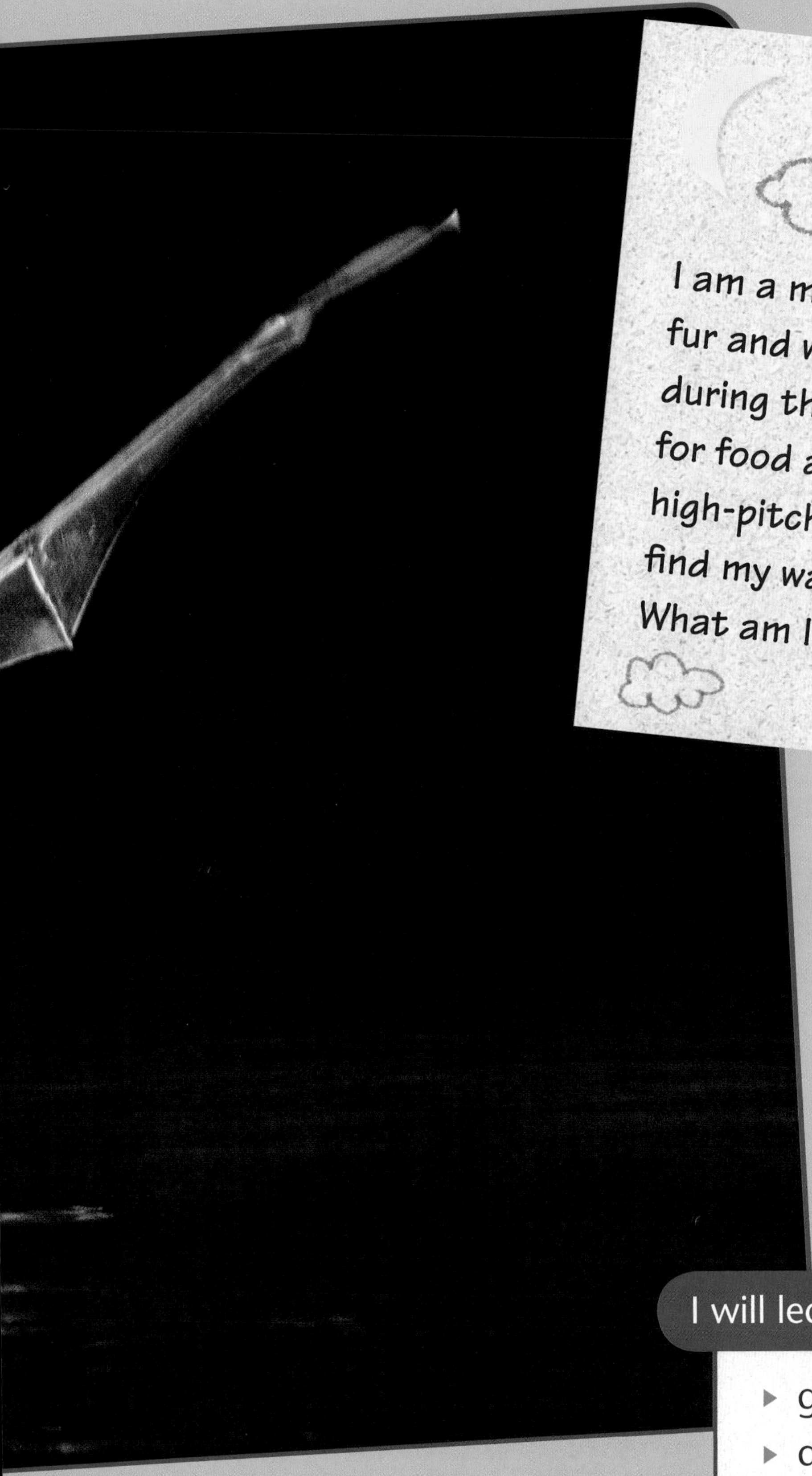

I am a mammal with both fur and wings. I sleep during the day, and I hunt for food at night. I use high-pitched sounds to find my way around.
What am I?

I will learn to talk about ...

- ▸ groups of animals
- ▸ animal characteristics
- ▸ animal habitats

Spotlight on Reading

Key Words

amphibian

bird

fish

mammal

reptile

Let's Predict!

▶ Answer the questions.

1. What does the title tell you about the passage?

2. What do the Key Words tell you about the passage?

3. What do the pictures tell you?

ANIMALS AROUND THE WORLD

by Tatiana Sildus

Animals live all over the world.
Different kinds of animals are able to live
in different climates and environments.
There are insects, birds, mammals, fish,
reptiles, and amphibians. Let's find out more
about these different kinds of animals.

Insects live everywhere, from tropical
forests to polar regions. All insects have three
pairs of legs and three body parts: the head,
the thorax, and the abdomen. Most insects
also have at least one pair of wings and
a pair of antennae. They lay eggs.

Birds live in all kinds of habitats, from cold mountains to hot deserts. Birds are warm-blooded animals with two legs, feathers, and a beak. All birds lay eggs and most can fly. Some birds, however, like penguins, cannot fly.

Mammals can live in different places, from prairies and oceans to big-city buildings. Most mammals give birth to live young. Then, they raise their babies on milk. Many mammals have fur or hair on their bodies. Humans, cats, dolphins, and whales are mammals.

Fish can be found in most bodies of water, from cold oceans to warm-water springs. All fish have gills for breathing. Many fish have scales for protection. Fins help fish swim better. All fish hatch from eggs.

Many reptiles live in the tropics and in deserts. Reptiles are cold-blooded animals. They need the warmth of the sun to keep their bodies warm. Their bodies are covered with dry, scaly skin. Most reptiles hatch from eggs that are laid on land.

Turtles, lizards, crocodiles, and alligators move
on short legs to get from one place to another.
Snakes crawl on their bellies to move around.
Many reptiles are also very good swimmers.

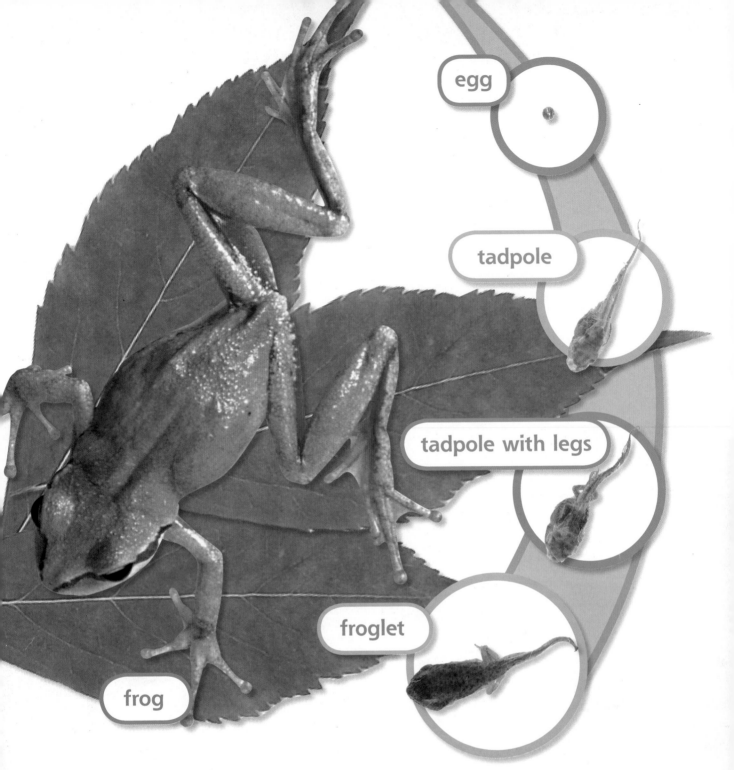

egg

tadpole

tadpole with legs

froglet

frog

Amphibians live in every continent
except Antarctica. When they are born, most
amphibians have gills and live in the water.
Then, they change into animals with lungs and
move to land. Amphibians have moist skin.
Frogs and salamanders are amphibians.

There are many different kinds of animals living all over the world.
What kinds of animals live in your area?

Let's Check!

A Answer the questions.

1. What three body parts do all insects have?

2. What birds cannot fly?

3. Which group of animals has fur or hair?

B Follow the directions.

1. Name each group of animal.

2. How is each animal different?

3. How is each animal the same?

Let's Summarize!

▶ Copy the animals graph. On the main legs of the graph, write the groups of animals mentioned in the passage. List three details about each group on the straight lines.

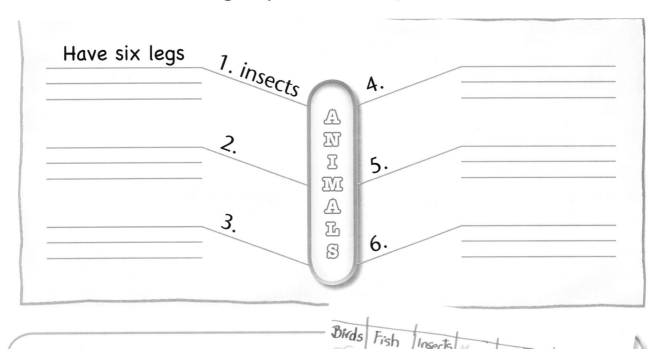

Have six legs

1. insects

2.

3.

A N I M A L S

4.

5.

6.

Let's Reflect!

Ⓐ Make an animal chart.

1. Draw six columns.

2. Label the columns Mammals, Reptiles, Amphibians, Birds, Fish, and Insects.

3. Draw and label these animals in the corresponding columns: shark, snake, dog, monkey, goldfish, frog, turtle, penguin, robin, butterfly, bat, bee, alligator.

Ⓑ Tell where each animal lives.

Spotlight on Language

Let's Connect!

A Listen and point to the animals.

Birds

Fish

Mammals

Reptiles

Key Words

climb
crawl
fly
run
swim
walk

B Describe how different animals can and cannot move.

Let's Focus!

▶ Copy and complete the sentences with words from the box.

| walk   crawl   swim   climb   fly   run |

1. Fish can _____. Fish cannot _____.

2. Cats can _____. Cats cannot _____.

3. Snakes can _____. Snakes cannot _____.

Let's Apply!

A Follow the instructions.

1. Draw your favorite bird, fish, mammal, and reptile.

2. Write two sentences about how each animal can and cannot move.

B Share your work with a classmate.

Let's Connect!

A Listen and read about how animals survive in their environment.

Goldfish have scales. Scales help fish protect their skin.

Goldfish also have gills. They breathe through their gills.

Goldfish have fins. Fins help fish swim quickly.

Bears have sharp teeth. They use their sharp teeth to eat fish.

Bears have thick fur. Fur keeps them warm.

Bears also have claws. They use their claws to get food and climb trees.

Woodpeckers have a beak. They use their beak to get food.

Woodpeckers have wings. Their wings let them fly.

Woodpeckers have feathers. Feathers keep birds warm and help them fly.

B Follow the directions.

1. Name two other animals that have fins.

2. Name two other animals that have fur.

3. Name two other animals that have feathers.

Let's Focus!

▶ Copy and complete the sentences.

> beak   feathers   fins   gills   scales   wings

1. Snakes have _____ .
   Snakes do not have _____ .

snake

2. Canaries have _____ .
   Canaries do not have _____ .

canary

3. Butterflies have _____ .
   Butterflies do not have _____ .

butterfly

4. Fish have _____ .
   Fish do not have _____ .

fish

Let's Apply!

▶ Answer the questions.

1. Why do some animals have fur?

2. Why do some animals have wings?

3. Why do some animals have teeth?

Let's Connect!

A Read the text.

African elephants are the largest land animals. They are also the heaviest land animals. An adult elephant is as heavy as twelve pick-up trucks!

Cheetahs are the fastest land animals. They can run as fast as cars on a highway!

Giraffes are the tallest land animals. Adult giraffes can be almost as tall as a two-story building!

B Answer the questions.

1. Which other land animals are large?

2. Which other land animals are tall?

3. Which other land animals are fast?

4. Which other land animals are heavy?

Let's Focus!

A Talk about these ocean animals.

BLUE WHALE

SEA HORSE

WHALE SHARK

B Choose the word that completes the sentence.

1. Blue whales are the (largest / large) animals in the ocean.

2. Whale sharks are the (longest / long) fish.

3. Sea horses are the (slow / slowest) swimmers.

Let's Apply!

▶ Follow the directions.

1. Choose three animals not mentioned in this unit. Draw and label them in your notebook.

2. Say which is the largest, the fastest, and the tallest of the three animals.

3. Write three sentences to compare your animals with each other.

Cinquain Poems

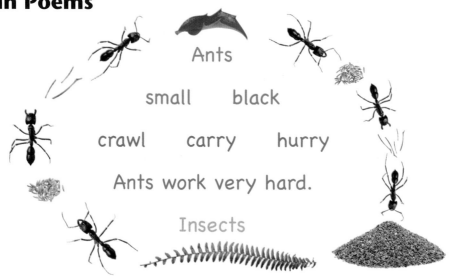

Ants

small   black

crawl   carry   hurry

Ants work very hard.

Insects

A Read this poem and compare it with the "Ants" poem.

Bird
White, gray
Flies, sings, swoops
Nests on rocky ledges
Gull

B Answer the questions.

1. Do these poems rhyme?

2. How many words does each line have?

3. Do you see a pattern in these poems?

4. How are these two poems the same?

Writing a Cinquain Poem

A cinquain is a poem that has five lines. These lines follow a specific pattern. Most cinquains have a specific number of syllables in each line. Some cinquains have a specific number of words in each line. Some cinquains have rhyme and others don't.

▶ Follow the steps for writing a cinquain poem.

1. Choose an animal.

2. Write two words that describe your animal.

big   small   tall   furry   scaly   short

3. Write three action words that describe what your animal does.

run   crawl   swim   fly   climb

4. Write a four-word phrase or complete sentence that describes your animal.

5. Write another word that tells what your animal is.

reptile   mammal   insect   bird   fish

Parts of Speech

Words that name a person, a place, or a thing are called **nouns**. The words *teacher, school, water, elephant,* and *insect* are nouns.

Words that describe a person, a place, or a thing are called **adjectives**. The words *happy, sad, big, small, fast, slow,* and *heavy* are adjectives.

Words that name an action are called **verbs**. The words *crawl, fly,* and *build* are verbs.

▶ Copy the chart. Write the words below in the correct column of the chart.

moths	jump	swim	interesting
raise	live	big	group
bird	red	nest	carry

nouns	verbs	adjectives

Multiplication

Multiplication is used to find fast answers when you need to add the same number again and again. Use the symbol × to show how many times you are multiplying a number.

Here are 3 groups of 5 monkeys.
This can be written 3 × 5.
Count by 5 to get the answer.

Here are 4 groups of 2 birds.
This can be written 4 × 2.
Count by 2 to get the answer.

Here are 2 groups of 10 fish.
This can be written 2 × 10.
Count by 10 to get the answer.

A Solve these addition problems. Count by 5, 10, or 2 to get each answer.

1. 5 + 5 + 5 + 5 = _____

2. 10 + 10 + 10 = _____

3. 2 + 2 + 2 + 2 + 2 + 2 = _____

B Change each of the above addition problems into a multiplication problem. Then, read the number sentences. For example, *5 + 5 + 5 is the same as 5 × 3.*

Social Studies

The American Bald Eagle

Every country has symbols that are important. Most countries use animals as official symbols because people can easily identify with them. The American bald eagle became an official U.S. symbol in 1782. Its picture is on the U.S. Great Seal, on postage stamps, and on U.S. currency. Bald eagles were chosen because they are big, strong, independent birds. Bald eagles are the largest birds in North America.

▶ Answer the questions.

1. Why are official symbols important?

2. Why do countries use animals as official symbols?

3. Where can you find the picture of the bald eagle?

4. What makes the bald eagle special?

Science Report

A science report gives written information and details about a scientific topic. To write a report, you must first do research to look up information about your topic. You can talk to your teacher, visit the library, or surf the Internet. Then, you will have facts and details to write your report.

▶ Write a science report.

1. Choose a scientific topic.

2. Use books, magazines, and the Internet to do your research.

3. Write the name of the topic as your title.

4. Write a first draft. Include a topic sentence, details that support the topic, and an ending sentence with your conclusion.

5. Circle and fix mistakes in your first draft with a colored pencil.

6. Write a final draft.

A Listen to the song.

The BEAR
WENT OVER THE MOUNTAIN

The bear went over the mountain
The bear went over the mountain
The bear went over the mountain
To see what he could see.

To see what he could see
To see what he could see
The bear went over the mountain
To see what he could see.

The other side of the mountain
The other side of the mountain
The other side of the mountain
Was all that he could see.

B Sing the song. Then, make up more verses to the song using the following animals and places.

fish/river   bird/tree   dolphin/ocean

Origami

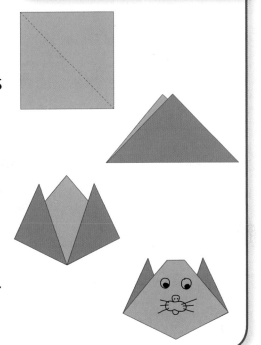

Origami is the art of paper folding. It is very popular in Japan. Origami paper is usually in the shape of a square. It comes in many different colors. Dinosaurs, birds, and many other animals are created by folding the paper in geometric patterns.

A Make an origami cat's head.

Supplies

- 6" x 6" piece of construction paper
- crayons or markers

Steps

1. Fold the paper in half to form a triangle.

2. Hold the paper triangle with the point at the top.

3. Fold each corner up to form ears on either side of the top point.

4. Turn the paper over so the ears are behind the head. Fold the top point back to make a flat top of the cat's head.

5. Draw a face on the front of your cat's head.

B Make your own origami figure. Write the steps to make that figure.

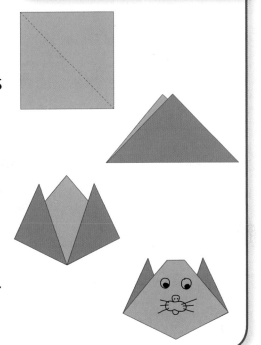

Impressions

★★★★ Pets in American Homes

More than half of all American families own pets. Pets are animals that live with people and keep them company. Many Americans think of their pets as family members. People may sign their pet's name on greeting cards, carry their pet's picture in their wallet, or even blow-dry their pet's hair after a bath! America has the highest number of homes with dogs and cats in the world.

These are the most popular pets in the United States: 1. cats, 2. dogs, 3. parakeets, 4. rabbits, 5. fish, and 6. hamsters.

A Answer the questions.

1. Do you like pets? Why or why not?

2. What do you think are the most popular pets in your country of origin?

B Copy and complete the chart.

1. Ask your classmates what pets they have.

2. Record their answers with tally marks.

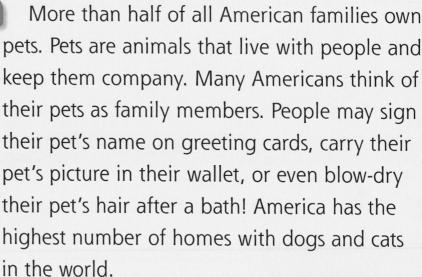

Pets Chart	
Cats	
Dogs	
Hamsters	
Rabbits	
Birds	
Fish	

A Make a poster about a place where animals live.

Supplies

- 1 large sheet of chart paper per group
- crayons or markers

Steps

1. Choose a habitat.

2. Research information about the habitat:
   - What does it look like?
   - What is the weather like?
   - What animals live there?
   - What plants grow there?

3. Write the name of the habitat at the top of the chart paper.

4. Draw the habitat.

5. Draw animals and plants that live in this habitat.

6. Label the animals and plants.

B Describe the animals that live in your habitat.

8 Heroes and Heroines

Mother **Teresa**
1910–1997

Martin **Luther King, Jr.**
1929–1968

Mahatma **Gandhi**
1869–1948

Oprah **Winfrey**
b. 1954

It can be a man, a woman, or a child.
It is someone who thinks of others first.
It is a person who is kind, strong,
and brave. Who is it?

eil **Armstrong**
b. 1930

I will learn to talk about ...

▸ heroes and heroines

▸ people in the past

▸ events in the past

Spotlight on Reading

Key Words

hero

play catch

baseball game

baseball bat

Let's Predict!

▶ Answer the questions.

1. What does the title tell you about the story?

2. What game is the girl going to play?

3. Who do you think her hero is? How can you tell?

Jackie's Gift

by Tatiana Sildus

Illustrated by Valeria Docampo

Jackie Robinson

It was a perfect day for baseball. The sun was shining in a bright blue sky. The kids at school had decided to get together for a ball game at the park today. I laced up my shoes, grabbed my bat, and ran out the door.

"Whoa! Take it easy, little one. Where are you going?"

I turned and saw my grandpa.

"My friends are playing baseball at the park!" I told him. "I'm going to play, too!"

When I got to the park, I saw the kids
from school playing catch. I ran over to
join them.

"Hey guys!" I said. "I came to play, too!"

"Sorry, Liz!" one of the kids said. "This game is for boys only. No girls are allowed!" I couldn't believe it. I had been looking forward to this game all week!

When I got home, Grandpa knew
something was wrong.

"Why are you back so soon?" he asked.

"They wouldn't let me play," I told him.

"They said the game was just for boys."

"Follow me, little one. I want to tell you
a story about my friend, Jackie."
Grandpa took my hand and led me down
to the basement.

He found a box high on a shelf. He took it down and pulled out an old picture.

"That's Jackie Robinson standing next to you!" I exclaimed. "You never told me you knew Jackie Robinson!"

Grandpa told me no one wanted to let
Jackie play baseball because he was black.
But Jackie didn't give up. He became a great
hero. Jackie gave the world a special gift.
He taught us that anything is possible when
you work hard and refuse to give up!

I ran back to the park.

"Come on, guys. Just give me a chance!"
I told my friends.

"Aw! Just let her play," one of the kids said.

I was so excited! We played all afternoon.
It was a great day. I will never forget the story
of Jackie's gift.

Let's Check!

A Answer the questions.

1. Where does the story take place?

2. Who is the main character in the story?

3. What is Liz's problem in the story?

4. How is her problem solved?

B Complete the sentences.

1. Liz goes to the park to _____.

2. On her way out, Liz sees _____.

3. The boys tell Liz she can't _____.

4. Liz's grandpa tells her the story of _____.

5. Liz persuades the boys to _____.

Let's Summarize!

▶ Look at the pictures. Write sentences to tell what Liz did and how she felt in the story.

Let's Reflect!

▶ Discuss the questions.

1. Why do you think the boys would not let Liz play baseball?

2. Do you think it was fair that Liz could not play? Why or why not?

3. Have you ever been in the same situation as Liz? Tell about it.

4. How was Liz's story and Jackie Robinson's story the same? How were they different?

Spotlight on Language

Let's Connect!

A Read from Liz's journal.

May 15

Today, the kids from school were playing baseball. I was excited because I wanted to play too, but the boys said I couldn't play. I felt very sad, until I talked to grandpa. Grandpa was looking through his things in the basement when he found a picture of Jackie Robinson.

Grandpa told me that Jackie Robinson was an important American hero because he never gave up. I listened to grandpa's story. Then, I decided I was going to try again. By the end of the day, I was playing baseball, too!

B Describe what the people in Liz's journal were doing.

Let's Focus!

▶ Complete the sentences with *was* or *were*.

1. The kids _____ playing catch.

3. Liz _____ reading a book.

2. Liz and her grandpa _____ playing a game.

4. Grandpa _____ reading the newspaper.

Let's Apply!

A Describe what was happening at school when you arrived this morning.

B Write a paragraph about what was happening this morning.

Let's Connect!

A Listen and point to the characters.

Key Words

allowed
became
gave
stayed
taught

B Follow the instructions.

1. Describe who Jackie Robinson was.

2. Tell why Jackie Robinson is remembered as an American hero.

Let's Focus!

A Choose the word that completes the sentence.

1. African Americans were not (allowed / gave) to play Major League Baseball.

2. Jackie Robinson (stayed / became) the first African-American player to play Major League Baseball.

3. Even though some people were mean to him, he (stayed / did) in the league and became a great player.

4. Jackie (went / gave) the world a special gift.

5. Jackie Robinson (taught / allowed) us that anything is possible if you work hard.

Let's Apply!

A Rewrite the sentences to talk about what Jackie Robinson did.

1. Jackie Robinson inspires other African-American players.

2. Jackie Robinson is a great baseball player.

3. Jackie Robinson teaches people to never give up.

B In the past, what great things did you do that made you feel proud?

Let's Connect!

▶ **Listen and read.**

I saw it! It was an excellent fastball.

Wow, he threw the ball very fast!

She batted really well! That was a great hit!

Yes, she swung the bat just in time. I thought girls couldn't play. I was wrong!

That was a fun game! Wasn't it?

Yes, it was. I had the best time today! I'm glad we let Liz play.

Bye, guys. I enjoyed playing baseball with you today.

Let's Focus!

▶ Rewrite the sentences to talk about what everyone did yesterday.

1. I walk to school.
2. They play baseball.
3. We watch movies.
4. He catches the ball.
5. I eat vegetables.
6. They have two books.
7. We write stories.

8. I drink orange juice.
9. She runs during the baseball game.
10. We read comic books.

Let's Apply!

▶ Think about three things you did yesterday.

1. Talk about the things you did.
2. Write a paragraph telling what you did.
3. Illustrate your paragraph.

Yesterday, I ran in the park.

A Biography

Sally Ride

Dr. Sally Ride is an important American heroine. She was born on May 26, 1951, in Encino, California. As a young girl, she loved to play tennis. Sally wanted to play professional tennis, but she decided to study science instead. In college, she decided to become an astronaut. She was the first American woman to go into space. Sally traveled in the Space Shuttle *Challenger* in 1983.

After she retired from being an astronaut, she became a professor and a children's book author. She is an inspiration to people everywhere!

▶ Read and answer the questions.

1. Is this story about a person, place, or thing?

2. Does this story seem real to you?

3. What kind of information does the text give you about the person in the story?

Writing a Biography

Biographies are written stories about a person's life. They tell about real people and actual events. They give facts about people's lives, including the time and place they were born, their accomplishments, and the impact they have had on others.

A Write a biography about a hero or heroine.

1. Choose a person you admire.

2. Do research about this person. Use these questions:
   - When was this person born?
   - What are some interesting facts about this person?
   - Why is this person a hero or heroine?

3. Write a biography.
   - Use the name of this person for the title.
   - Include a topic sentence.
   - Write the facts about this person.
   - Include an ending sentence.

B Illustrate your biography.

Regular and Irregular Verbs

Regular Verbs

Present	Past
jump	jumped
play	played
walk	walked
watch	watched

Add -ed to the end of most action words when talking about a past event that is not ongoing.

Common Irregular Verbs

Present	Past
eat	ate
drink	drank
has	had
read	read
run	ran
write	wrote

Many action words are irregular. We do not add -ed. We just need to learn what the past form of the action word is.

▶ Follow the instructions.

1. Make a list of ten action words.

2. Write the past form of each word.

3. Draw the action word.

Word Problems with Time

To tell how long something lasts, you can use two clocks to count and compare the hours and minutes. Remember that the small hand tells the hour, while the big hand tells the minutes. There are five minutes between each of the numbers on a clock. To count how long something lasts, add the hours and minutes between the beginning time and the ending time.

▶ Answer the questions.

Mary's soccer game starts at 8:00 a.m. It ends at 5:00 p.m.

John's soccer game starts at 8:00 a.m. It ends at 3:00 p.m.

1. How long will Mary be at her game?

2. How long will John be at his game?

3. Which game is longer, John's or Mary's?

The Founding Fathers

The Founding Fathers of the United States were great heroes. They helped found our nation, the United States of America. Some, like George Washington, participated in the American Revolution as leaders. Others, like Thomas Jefferson, wrote and signed the Declaration of Independence. This document declares the United States of America a free and independent country. The Founding Fathers are heroes because they worked hard to make our country free and safe.

▶ Answer the questions.

1. What is the Declaration of Independence?

2. Who was a leader of the American Revolution?

3. Why are freedom and safety important?

4. Why are the Founding Fathers considered heroes?

Social Studies

Pasteurization

Louis Pasteur often wondered why milk spoiled so quickly. He thought that bacteria were causing the milk to spoil. He boiled milk to kill the bacteria. He compared it with a milk sample that was not boiled. After doing this experiment many times, he concluded that the boiled milk lasted longer than the other milk. This process is called *pasteurization*.

Louis Pasteur was a famous French scientist. He was born on December 27, 1822. Pasteur discovered the process of pasteurization and developed vaccines for several diseases, including rabies. Pasteur was honored by the French government for his contributions to saving lives.

▶ Answer the questions.

1. What did Pasteur think caused milk to spoil so quickly?

2. What did Pasteur do to test his idea?

3. What was his conclusion?

4. Why is the process called *pasteurization*?

A Listen to the song.

Remembering American Heroes and Heroines

American heroes, American heroines,
long ago, long ago.
Some were fighting injustice,
some were curing diseases,
helping you, helping me.

American heroes, American heroines,
long ago, long ago.
Some were men and women,
some were little children,
helping you, helping me.

American heroes, American heroines,
long ago, long ago.
We'll never forget them,
we'll try to be like them,
helping you, helping me.

Jonas Salk

Abraham Lincoln

Ruby Nell Bridges

B Sing the song.

C Choose a hero or heroine from the photos on the page.
Create and sing the last verse about the person you chose.

Portraits

Francis Luis Mora

A portrait is a picture of a person. A portrait can be taken with a camera. It can also be painted or drawn. Francis Luis Mora was a famous portrait painter from Uruguay. He loved to paint people in outdoor scenes. People all over the world collect his work.

A Paint a portrait of your favorite hero or heroine.

Steps	Supplies

Steps

1. Choose a hero or heroine and paint his or her portrait.

2. Paint the outline of your hero's face. Then fill it in with color that looks like his or her skin.

3. Paint your hero's hair, eyes, lips, nose, and mouth.

4. Paint the top of your hero's shirt or dress.

Supplies

- construction paper (18" x 18")
- paint
- paintbrushes
- painter's smock or old T-shirt

B Describe your portrait.

Those Who Help Others

There are many people who have spent their lives helping others. Some are heroes or heroines because they work for peace. Some work hard to make sure everyone has the same chance to succeed in life. Some help those who are sick or dying.

Martin Luther King, Jr., fought for equal rights for African Americans.

Eunice Kennedy Shriver has helped people with disabilities.

Mother Teresa helped thousands of people in India who were sick and dying.

Gandhi led peaceful protests to free India from the rule of the British Empire.

Oprah Winfrey has created schools in Africa so that girls can get an education and succeed in life.

A Talk about someone you consider a hero or heroine from your country of origin.

B What can you do to help others in your school, your community, and your world?

Heroes and Heroines in History

A Help create a class timeline of heroes and heroines.

Steps

1. Make a class list of heroes and heroines.

2. Choose one person from the list.

3. Learn three interesting facts about this person. Write them down.

4. Create a bulletin board and title it "Our Heroes and Heroines."

5. Make a line across the bulletin board.

6. Use pushpins to place the pictures of your class heroes and heroines and their birth dates on the timeline.

Supplies

- bulletin board
- paper
- pushpins
- pictures of heroes and heroines
- markers

= Our Heroes and Heroines =

1732   1910   1929   1935   1963

B Discuss with a classmate.

1. How does a person become a hero or heroine?

2. What can you do to be a hero or heroine?

A

amphibian

bathroom

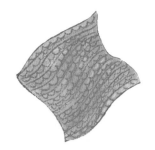

blanket

B

baby

beak

blouse

baseball bat

bedroom

bus driver

baseball game

bird

C

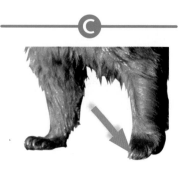

claws

cloudy

crib

dumpster

D

coach

dad

dusting

cooking

desert

E

eraser

crayon

doctor

excited

exercise

fins

food server

eyes

fire station

forest

F

family

firefighter

fruit

feathers

fish

fur

grocer

heroine

instruments

grocery store

hospital

kitchen

hair

inline skates

lake

hero

insect

librarian

library

mayor

mountain

living room

meal

N

nervous

M

mail carrier

milk

nurse

mammal

mom

O

ocean

pajamas

plant

poster

park

play catch

principal

pencil

player

race car

planet

police officer

rainy

reptile

scared

security guard

river

school

skirt

ruler

school bus

snowy

scales

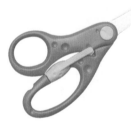

scissors

soccer

sweater

vacuuming

watercolors

T

team

volcano

windy

teeth

W

washing dishes

wings

toys

water